A Teen's Guide to Conflict

How to Deal with Drama,

Manage Anger, and

Make Things Right

Gary Chapman

with Jennifer Thomas and Paige Haley Drygas

NORTHFIELD PUBLISHING

CHICAGO

Some content is adapted from material previously published by Gary Chapman, Jennifer Thomas, and Paul White.

Some names and details have been changed to protect the privacy of individuals, while some are fictitious or composites for the sake of illustration.

Produced with the assistance of Peachtree Publishing Services.

Edited by Pamela Joy Pugh
Cover design: Brittany Schrock
Interior design: Erik M. Peterson and Brandi Davis
Interior graphic of bomb copyright © 2025 by Kiselov/Adobe Stock (308589903). Interior graphic of pop art background copyright © 2025 by ahmad/Adobe Stock (773296720). Interior graphic of speech bubbles copyright © 2025 by Viktoria/Adobe Stock (639402775). All rights reserved.

Library of Congress Cataloging-in-Publication Data

Names: Chapman, Gary D., 1938- author. | Drygas, Paige, author. | Thomas, Jennifer, 1969- author.
Title: A teen's guide to conflict : how to deal with drama, manage anger, and make things right / Gary Chapman, Paige Drygas, Jennifer Thomas.
Description: Chicago : Northfield Publishing, [2025] | Includes bibliographical references. | Audience: Ages teens | Audience: Grades 10-12 | Summary: "Relationships matter. But conflict can lead to isolation, anger, and broken relationships. With the proper tools, teenagers can learn to respond to conflict and experience meaningful community. This book helps teenagers tame the powerful emotion of anger, apologize (and receive apologies) in ways that work, and handle difficult relationships"-- Provided by publisher.
Identifiers: LCCN 2024059857 (print) | LCCN 2024059858 (ebook) | ISBN 9780802435309 (paperback) | ISBN 9780802470447 (ebook)
Subjects: LCSH: Anger--Religious aspects--Christianity. | Anger in children--Religious aspects--Christianity. | Children--Conduct of life.
Classification: LCC BV4627.A5 C49 2025 (print) | LCC BV4627.A5 (ebook) | DDC 248.8/3--dc23/eng/20250216
LC record available at https://lccn.loc.gov/2024059857
LC ebook record available at https://lccn.loc.gov/2024059858

We hope you enjoy this book from Northfield Publishing.
Our goal is to provide high-quality, thought-provoking books and products that connect truth to your real needs and challenges. For more information on other books and products that will help you with all your important relationships, go to 5lovelanguages.com or write to:

Northfield Publishing
820 N. LaSalle Blvd.
Chicago, IL 60610
1 3 5 7 9 10 8 6 4 2

Printed in the United States of America

Gary
Dedicated to every teen who would like to make the world a better place by building healthy relationships.

Jennifer
To every teen who already senses that it's the quality of our relationships that governs our personal fulfillment in life.

Paige
To all the teens out there who are making the world a better place, starting with their own relationships.
And to those teens who make me smile every day: my two sons and my 112 students.

·

Contents

Prologue

"All the world's a stage,
And all the men and women merely players."
—William Shakespeare, *As You Like It*

Sometimes life just feels like that: a play on a stage, and you're an actor in costume, playing a role in the grand drama unfolding around you. You know your lines, you recite them smoothly, you play your part . . . until you don't.

Sometimes the other actors seem crazed, the set falls apart, you forget your lines, your costume has a hole in it, you hate your assigned role, and life feels more like an out-of-control drama than a well-rehearsed play.

Welcome to life: unscripted, full of conflict, the director backstage and sometimes far from our limited human view, and a rolling act of improv spinning around us.

The purpose of this book is to help you deal with the inevitable drama of life, manage your simmering anger, make things right when you invariably fall off the stage, and grow in the process. You'll find the chapters in this book organized progressively so that they build from one to the next, but if you spot a topic and need specific advice *right now,* then flip forward and read away. The sections in the book are titled Acts, and the chapters are Scenes. (Get it? Life is drama!)

And now, reader, may you learn and grow in this process with us as we share tips and stories from the thousands of real people just like you that we—Dr. Jennifer Thomas and I—have worked with in our role as counselors. Their lives aren't perfect, but they've learned to live out their "strange eventful history" (Shakespeare again) and live it to the fullest (Jesus this time; check out John 10:10).

—Dr. Gary Chapman

Act 1

DEALING WITH DRAMA

SCENE 1

Common Conflicts

When we hear the word *conflict*, most of us have negative conno-
tations. In our minds, conflict = bad. Sometimes that's true.
Some conflicts are negative and painful.

Some conflicts are healthy, though. In a movie or book, there is
no plot without conflict. If every character swims merrily along, then
nothing actually happens in the story. If Katniss doesn't challenge
the Capitol, the story fades after the reaping. If Hamlet doesn't face
down his murderous uncle/stepdad, or if the Avengers don't rally
together to fight Thanos, then the villain wins unchallenged.

Conflict can stretch us. On a sports team, a coach often pits players against one another, competing for playing time and sharpening
each other's skills. That's good conflict. In a friendship, if one person
disagrees and is able to voice that in a healthy way, that's good conflict. When handled well, those good conflicts lead to growth. The
team gets better. The friendship gets stronger. The individuals grow.

But some conflicts are unhealthy, and often, we struggle to discern
between good and bad conflicts—and we have no idea how to address
either type. For many of us, conflicts feel like quicksand, dragging us
down, drowning us up to our eyeballs and overwhelming our senses.

How we handle conflicts will make or break our relationships. Our
goal is to provide a framework for understanding relational difficulties
and to offer tools to manage them effectively. Attempting to build
a conflict-free life is not realistic or even desirable. Differences are
critical to our growth as individuals. We need friends with different

perspectives, personalities, communication styles, and life experiences. Those kinds of friends complement and stretch us. If we isolate ourselves in a bubble and only interact with people who think/talk/live exactly like us, then we stagnate.

However, too much conflict or drama can become toxic, a drain on our energy, and a block in our growth. We want to help you correctly understand disagreements and navigate relational challenges so you can prevent, or at least minimize, the escalation of festering conflicts.

Every relationship involves conflict. By definition, relationships are dynamic, fluid, and ever-changing because they're the unique interaction between people. Most relationships are based on some commonality: for example, a common goal (those beloved/dreaded group projects in school), a common time or space (coworkers at the grocery or Chick-fil-A), common interests (lacrosse team or marching band or robotics club). We choose some of our relationships, such as our friends. Others seem to happen to us, such as our parents, siblings, teachers, or coworkers. Whatever form our relationships take, we all need to be in relationship in order to truly flourish. No person grows well in isolation.

This is the fabric of life. We are all in relationships, we all face conflicts, and we all have to learn how to navigate them so that we, and our relationships, can truly thrive.

Why Conflict?

Where does conflict even come from? Let's zero in on actual people and offenses. Like any good problem-solving, specifying what the actual "problem" is and its root cause is the first step.

Meet Cole. Cole's English teacher snaps impatiently at him when he stays after class to ask for help on his argumentative essay. He does not understand her feedback on his last piece of writing, he feels anxious about earning a better grade on this essay (imagine fire-breathing parents), and she has invited students to schedule writing conferences with her.

Cole needs to remember that the symptoms (Mrs. Jackson's rudeness) are not necessarily the problem. When your back aches, you can take painkillers, but until you address the issue actually causing the pain, like a pinched nerve or pulled muscle, the symptoms will likely return.

What is the actual problem? Cole may never know that Mrs. Jackson spent last night in the ER with her son, who snapped his collarbone at football, and she's worried about how to pay for his upcoming visit with the orthopedic surgeon. He may notice the dark circles under her eyes and the extra-venti coffee on her desk but not realize how exhausted she is. He can't control any of those issues.

What can Cole control? Did he submit his last three essays late? Has he established a pattern of complaining about his grades? Does he even look at her feedback on his previous work before submitting a fresh essay? Does he arrive to class on time? Does he treat her respectfully, or does he play games on his laptop while she's giving the class instructions? All of those are relational factors that can taint their interactions, and all of those are within Cole's control.

If Cole has done everything in his power to uphold his end, then he may need to give her a little grace and space, wait a day, and send her a polite follow-up email. And he cannot take her impatient reaction personally. Sometimes that's easier said than done but, like the duck, we have to learn to let most water roll right off our backs.

The Relationship Continuum

We also need to remind ourselves that having problems with someone is not an all-or-nothing experience. We do not have to resort to extremes: "I love that teacher" vs. "I hate that teacher." Or "That friend is my closest confidant" vs. "That former friend is now dead to me." (Honestly, we can all be a touch extreme.) The quality and level of our relationships exists on a *continuum,* as do the challenges in those relationships. Some people irritate us. Others we really enjoy, but only up to a point, and then we need a break from them. A few people are easy and effortless to be around.

We seem to be able to communicate clearly and naturally with some people, while other people mystify us, and they don't seem to get us. Understanding another human takes a lot of time and energy. We might sigh and wonder, "Is it even worth it?"

Is it? Let's visualize a team of twenty players. On that team, let's say you become close friends with two; you really click. Most of the team may always hover in the acquaintance category: you never feel close to them, but you figure out how to work well together. Then maybe there are two who rub you the wrong way because you're wired opposite in terms of personality and communication style. You tolerate each other, but you wouldn't choose to sit together on a road trip. Then there's one player whom you actively dislike because of some unresolved conflict that clouds the relationship. (We can work on that.) And finally, you may have a rare person who doesn't feel safe because of a history of betrayal, and you wisely choose to minimize your contact with that player. Notice the range of relationships on that one team. That's typical of life.

Misunderstanding + Miscommunication

Some conflicts boil down to simple misunderstandings or miscommunications. Sometimes we *mishear* people: literally, we do not accurately hear what the other person said. Cole's English teacher may have told him to "bring a completed draft of your essay during activity period," and he may have heard her say she "won't look at a completed draft, period." Big difference.

We can also fall in the trap of *misinterpreting* the message that someone is sending us. Cole's teacher may have wanted him to bring her a completed draft to respond to because she thinks that will help him the most in the writing process, but he is so stuck on his outline that he can't even begin to write the draft. He misinterprets her willingness to help him; he thinks she won't. And she thinks he is unwilling to do what she has asked, which is a misinterpretation.

Their dual misinterpretation is a comedy of errors, but it feels more like a frustrating tragedy.

The skill of active listening can help us avoid this trap. Try closing out a conversation with a clarifying statement. After an intense conversation with her coach after practice, Mckenna summarizes, "What I hear you saying is that you want me to work on my 1v1 defending and winning balls out of the air. Is that right, Coach?" The coach now has the chance to confirm or clarify. Communication success.

Flat-Out Differences

Some conflicts are the result of natural differences with others: different perspectives, opinions, and preferences. This is normal, and even healthy. If a player can only play for one style of coach, it doesn't bode well for the athlete's future. If a student can only perform on a multiple-choice test, that limitation will hurt her academically. We have to learn to be flexible and begin to recognize that some of our relational conflicts are the result of innocent differences of opinion or style and are simply not worth fighting over.

Clashing Personalities

Some people simply rub us the wrong way. They aren't doing anything wrong; they are just so different. We have distinct personality styles and communication patterns. Have you ever taken a personality test (or several)? These tests sort personality traits into a myriad of categories, such as interpersonal energy: introversion vs.

extroversion; invisible motivations that drive behaviors, such as the Enneagram; cultural orientations like individualism vs. collectivism; and so on. These tests aren't measuring right vs. wrong traits. They simply help us understand ourselves and others better.

Consider the curious case of Kate and Laila, her boyfriend Drew's mom. Kate has grown up in a family where communication is polite but very direct. People say what they mean. They're kind but straight-up honest. When Kate started dating Drew, she sometimes shocked him with her honesty, though he found it refreshing. He always knows exactly where he stands with her. Drew's mom, Laila, however, grew up in a very different culture. She is an equally kind person but communicates in an opposite style: soft and indirect. Neither style is right or wrong—they're just different.

When Kate says, "Would y'all like to come over for our Fourth of July party?" what she means is "You are invited and welcome." It's a straightforward invitation meant to be taken at face value.

Laila can't decide what to think: *Is there actually space for us? Is this a token invitation? Do they really want our family to come? Surely it's an imposition, isn't it? If they really mean it, won't they follow up and ask again?* An indirect communicator at heart, Laila replies, "Oh, we couldn't possibly come." What she wants is reassurance that Kate's family wants them to come; what Kate hears is they can't come, so she drops it. They're both speaking English, but they are not speaking the same language. Communication failure.

Feeling Disrespected

Most of us are too touchy. We get offended far too easily. A word of caution for all of us: When you feel that initial flash of offense, don't go nuclear. Don't assume the worst of the other person. Each of us carries around weights of unspoken expectations, and each of us can find ten or one hundred little opportunities to feel offended every day. If at all possible, don't.

People are sensitive to different things. (Side note: If you haven't yet, read *A Teen's Guide to the 5 Love Languages* for more details on how to understand yourself and others on a deeper level.) Someone who values Time may feel offended if she's not invited with a group of friends to go get smoothies after practice. A person who values Words may feel more sensitive when the director stops the entire rehearsal to single him out for feedback, especially if that director uses an intense tone. The director may think she's showing the musician respect; the student may take the feedback way too personally.

Conflict Resolution

We live in a world where too many conflicts are "resolved" through violence, or behind the anonymity and vicious tone of the internet, or by simply discarding every relationship that gets the tiniest bit difficult. But **what if**? **What if** we all learned to resolve conflict more effectively? **What if** we learned to work through conflict, rather than lash out in anger? **What if** we took the time to repair our fractured relationships? **What if** we became brave enough to extend the olive branch of peace? **What if** we learned to see the humanity in others and chose to love rather than hate? **What if** we assumed the best in others, rather than the worst?

For the rest of this book, let's explore that magical **what if**.

Reflection

- In your mind, is all conflict bad? Can there be good/healthy conflict that makes you better? Give examples.

- Have you ever experienced a team dynamic in which everyone got along and there was zero conflict? If so, do you think that was genuine—meaning, everyone liked each other and was truly at peace—or was the surface "peace" due to an avoidance of conflict?

- Think about your own personality. What types of people do you tend to struggle with? Why do you think that is? In your experience, have you been able to improve those relationships over time, and if so, how?

- In your opinion, how realistic is it to expect a lack of conflict in all your relationships? Is there an acceptable level of conflict or tension for you? Describe.

- Why do you think most of us get offended so easily?

SCENE 2

Communication Skills

The day Santiago tore his ACL felt like the worst day of his life. His dominant season: gone. His dreams of being recruited for college: vanishing. His central role as the captain of his team: replaced. His mental health: crushed.

At first Santiago's team was incredibly supportive. Several friends showed up at the hospital on the day of his surgery. A few came over to play video games with him and keep him company while he was immobilized and recovering. The supportive messages flowed in, and then . . . gradually . . . silence.

He had played with these guys for years. Were they still his friends now that he couldn't play? One of the newer players took his starting spot and was playing out of his mind. Did they even need him, let alone remember him? Was it personal, or were they just busy?

The team sensed Santiago's discomfort, so they tried to give him space. They didn't want him to feel like they were rubbing it in his face when they played a big game, especially when they won without him. They created a separate text string that didn't include him so they wouldn't disturb him.

And the silence felt deafening to Santiago.

Not all conflicts are the result of major events that cause serious relational ruptures. In fact, many, maybe even most, relational difficulties in our homes, on our teams, and with our friends stem from minor glitches that can be addressed through some practical strategies. If we can learn to improve our communication skills, then we can avoid the majority of disagreements and conflicts that, like pesky weeds, are just waiting to sprout if we ignore or avoid them. In other words, if we can be proactive in our relationships so that conflicts don't explode, then we won't have to go through the more intense process of repairing broken relationships. As the ancient saying goes, "An ounce of prevention is better than a pound of cure." All in favor of some easy prevention strategies?

These five communication skills can help you avoid a flood of unnecessary conflicts:

1. Check for understanding with active listening.
2. Clarify misperceptions, misinterpretations, and misattributions of motives.
3. Commit to direct communication (vs. indirect).
4. Avoid deception, in all its sneaky forms.
5. Accept that others view the world differently than you—and that's okay.

Here's the guarantee on the side of the box: If you build these five behaviors into your daily interactions, you'll see the number and intensity of your disagreements plummet.

Can You Hear Me?

Who's good at multitasking? Did every reader raise a hand?

False! We humans tell ourselves that we can multitask: texting, social media, homework, music, conversation, family dinner, show in the background, everything all at once. It's a sloppy habit that most of us are guilty of. But the truth is that humans, unlike computers, have singular wiring. We can do one task (well) at a time.

At the pace at which most of us live, trying to do seven things at once, with constant background noise and distractions, we set ourselves up for relational misunderstandings. We can prevent a slew of conflicts simply by slowing down, shutting off distractions, and devoting our full attention to the speaker.

Experiment today. When someone wants to talk to you, consciously turn your phone face down, and mute all other distractions. Give the speaker both of your ears and both of your eyes. Don't rush the speaker along by completing his sentences. Offer him the gift of your undivided attention. Listen completely.

I Think I Heard You Say . . .

After you listen well, check for understanding. Summarize what the speaker said and what, if anything, is being asked of you. This works wonders to simmer down conflicts.

Consider the following scenarios and pick the best response.

Case study 1: The director feels frustrated with the entire cast and crew, who came to rehearsal unprepared and unfocused. She pulls a small group of the veterans aside and vents on you all, which maybe isn't the most professional response, but you can see where she's coming from. You collectively were an artistic disaster today. Which response defuses the conflict?

A. "Ms. Smith, relax. We have a full month till opening night. We'll be fine; we always are."

B. "Okay, okay, we get it, Ms. Smith. Just move on already."

C. "Ms. Smith, I hear you saying that this was a weak rehearsal. We agree. You want us to set today aside and come back tomorrow with a different level of focus."

Case study 2: Your dad is planning to take the Jeep to Home Depot. He storms back into the house furious: the gas tank is empty, the back seat is filled with empty Gatorade bottles, and the floor is covered in mud and turf pellets. The Jeep is trashed. Your dad demands to know: Is this your work, or your older brother's? Conveniently, your brother is out with friends, so he's an easy target. Which response defuses the conflict?

A. "Not me. That must have been Jack. Plus I drive the Jeep the least, and it's not that bad, Dad."

B. "Seriously, Dad, your idea of taking turns cleaning the Jeep will never work. Forget about it."

C. "Dad, I'm sorry the Jeep is a mess. I don't know if it was Jack or me or some combination, but I understand why you feel frustrated. I hear you saying that you want us to take more responsibility to clean the Jeep, and that seems fair."

Empathy works wonders. If you chose script C for each case study, you just defused the bomb before it exploded.

Even when you don't fully agree with the speaker, you can validate their views. The practice of restating others' arguments, especially when you think they are wrong, requires maturity and practice.

Communication Tips

Scan this list of communication tips. Do these seem obvious? Are you nodding your head? That's a great sign. Let's make sure to consistently apply these techniques when conflicts spark:

> Be respectful. (Try a Southern-style "sir" or "ma'am" on an irritated adult. Works magic.)
> Convey gratitude. ("Thanks, Dad, for letting us drive the Jeep.")
> Show interest in others' ideas; the universe doesn't revolve around you.
> Even when you disagree—*especially* when you disagree—repeat back what the speaker said to show that you get it. (All-pro tip: If the speaker keeps repeating herself, that may be your

clue that she doesn't think you get what she's saying.)
Add humor, when appropriate. Most of life isn't WWIII. Acting
moody makes problems seem bigger. Being positive can
reset the tone of a conversation.

If you're in a tough conversation with a defensive or hostile speaker,
then do *not* . . .

Physically escalate the conflict (pointing a finger, raising the
volume, slamming a door, crossing your arms to convey
defensiveness, etc.).

Take personal shots. Resist it!

Use extreme words such as *always*, *none*, and *never*. We abuse
superlatives. ("This is the worst family in the history of the
world!" Really? No, not really.)

Blame others.

Make excuses for yourself.

Mock and smirk.

Escalate the argument in front of others, drawing them into
the fray and making the speaker feel cornered.

Yes? *Yes.* If we can learn to consistently apply these communication
skills, then we can neutralize a ton of conflicts before they fester or
escalate. Then we can save our energy for more important things in life.

Back to Santiago at the start of this chapter: At the end of the
season, when Santiago had fully recovered from his ACL injury, he
faced a tough choice. Should he stay with his longtime team, who had
seemingly iced him, or find a new team and start fresh? His answer
will likely depend on how well he communicated with his team, and
how well they kept him engaged. Could his entire future in sports
come down to . . . communication?

Reflection

- What does multitasking look like in your life? We all do it, so let's come clean. What tasks do you try to do all at once? Honestly reflect on how this affects the quality of your communication.

- Describe a friend who's a strong communicator. What does he or she do that makes you feel heard?

- Assuming you buy the premise of this chapter (that we can prevent a ton of little conflicts simply by communicating better), think of a recent mini-conflict in your life that you could have defused earlier, before the spark ignited into a wildfire. What simple things could you have done differently?

- Humans love to make excuses. Check out Adam and Eve in Genesis 3. This is the first conflict in human history, and it turns into a game of hot potato: "She made me do it!" "No, it was that sneaky snake!" How do you react when someone disappoints you and then makes a lame excuse?

- Scan back over the two lists of tips (the Dos and Don'ts). Think about the conflicts in your family of origin. Where do those usually fall apart?

SCENE 3

Dangerous Assumptions

This is a story about assuming the worst of someone.

When Luke's dad got fired, their family's world seemed to collapse. He had a high-profile job as a varsity basketball head coach in a sports-obsessed town. For years he had been revered, maybe in an almost unhealthy way, but was that his fault? He knew everyone, had connections, and seemed to float through life, untouchable. He won games, he lost games, he developed all-star players, he hired assistants, he built a program. Some people loved him.

Some people hated him.

A few parents went vigilante on him. One player was no longer getting the playing time his parents were sure he deserved, so those parents, aggressive and entitled to the core, set their sights on the coach. They did not want their son's "rightful" playing time; they wanted the coach's blood. They did not meet with the coach. Instead, they met with the superintendent. They met with the school board. They picked off the trainer and the assistant coaches, one by one. They collected "evidence" and framed it in the worst possible light. They recruited a few other disgruntled parents, and the sparks fanned into a raging fire.

The coach was fired.

Was he perfect? No. He had made mistakes. He had favored some players and underestimated others, and he had lost some games that he should have won. But he hadn't done anything criminal, and he had done his best. The bloodthirsty parents never had a candid, direct conversation with the coach. They just attacked.

Then gossip spread like wildfire, and Luke was the next burn victim. Just as parents had turned on the coach, so some students turned on Luke, starting with the team. They assumed the worst of Luke:

"You only got playing time because of your dad."

"Classic case of nepotism."

"You need to leave. The team and the school."

"Your dad must have done something terrible to get himself fired."

"You're as toxic as your dad."

"Like father, like son."

The same message, in a dozen subtle and not-so-subtle forms: "Leave."

The parents assumed the worst of the coach, the team assumed the worst of Luke, and the collateral damage was one man's career and his son's ability to trust.

Snap Judgments

Negative assumptions about others are one of the most serious, insidious threats to relationships and are a root cause of many conflicts. These are the stories we tell ourselves internally. Often they're false, and when they're false, they seriously hurt our relationships. Let's demystify some of these automatic stories that lead to catastrophic relationship breakdowns.

Our brains have a protective mode that helps us make split-second judgments about time, distance, and safety. Most of these snap judgments are right—but not all. New drivers learn how to process all the data in front of them (for example, the proximity of other cars, their relative speed, road conditions, traffic flow, that erratic driver to the left, reported speed trap ahead) and make quick decisions about when to accelerate, when to brake, and when to change lanes to get away from that swerving car in the left lane. These protective decisions literally save our physical lives. Our brains naturally apply those same survival instincts to relationships. Sometimes our instincts are right, like sensing that you should avoid a creepy stranger. But sometimes we assume the worst of others, without any evidence, and that can be disastrous. When we misjudge others, when we mislabel their motives, when we assume that others dislike us, when we react with mistrust because of our own baggage, we erode our relationships.

Warped Assumptions

Just ask Brody. He recently started working at a pizza restaurant—not the most glamorous job, but it pays well enough and has flexible hours. The manager told him she was impressed with how quickly he was learning their systems. She told him that the "big three" (the owner and the two managers) had noticed him already. At first Brody felt flattered. "I'm glad they're watching," he thought. But then he started to question the manager's motives, even though she had given him no reason to distrust her. "Does she tell every new employee that? I wonder if the owner gives her a script. Is she really just trying to manipulate me so I'll work more hours?" Brody's reaction reflects his own mistrust and doesn't lead anywhere good.

While it's tempting, we should not assume the worst of others. Our culture has an aura of cynicism. It's easy to look at the world and see everything that's broken, but that's a toxic way to live. Our learned cynicism can undermine our relationships.

That cynicism infected Piper's new friendships. When Piper was invited to join a group of friends for homecoming, she felt elated. She was new to the school and trying to find her place in the social strata. But negative thoughts intruded. "Do they even want me there, or are they just using me for my house for the after-party? Do they even know me well enough to genuinely like me? Did the counselor tell them they had to include me? Sienna's mom works with my mom; maybe she made them invite me." As Piper's cynicism got louder, she withdrew from her friends. She got icy cold toward the group and eventually pulled away completely. She skipped homecoming. While there's nothing morally wrong with missing the homecoming dance, and in some cases that might be a wise decision, in Piper's case, she missed out on a chance to make lasting memories with her new friends simply because she assumed the worst of them, without any evidence to support her fears.

It is really hard to sift through everything in our own hearts and minds, let alone someone else's. In fact, "The heart is deceitful above all things and beyond cure. Who can understand it?" (Jeremiah 17:9 NIV). This is not a rhetorical question: Who can fully understand the human heart? Only God (see Jeremiah 17:10). If we can't fully understand our own hearts, then how can we possibly know someone else's hidden thoughts and tangled motives? Too often, we assume the worst. "They want to make me look bad. They're trying to edge me out. Did you hear their tone? They have a hidden agenda." Our minds go there too fast!

The remedy? Assume the best in others, until they give us hard evidence that they cannot be trusted, and communicate directly with them, rather than through hints and subtext.

Hard Conversations

Gracie and Bella have been the school newspaper editors for two years. When their journalism teacher retired, they held their breath, waiting to see who the new teacher would be. Mrs. Perez landed. She was fiery and fun, just what their program needed, but she had a different style than the former teacher. More visionary, less organized. More vocal, less empowering. And she seemed to be pitting Gracie and Bella against each other in a strange battle. She clearly favored Gracie and gave her more responsibility. She praised her in front of the staff (with no mention of Bella) and pulled her aside to make important decisions (without Bella). It was as if Bella no longer mattered.

Bella naturally felt excluded. The thoughts flitted through her mind: "Did Gracie start this? She must love being the favorite, right? What is she saying about me behind my back?"

Bella stood at a fork in the road: Assume the worst of Gracie, which would have been easy, and pull back slowly? Or have a conversation directly with Gracie? "This is what I'm feeling and perceiving. What do you see? Do you have any suggestions for me? I can't control Mrs. Perez, but I don't want this to come between us and ruin our friendship."

Hard as it was to start that conversation, Bella bravely talked to her friend, and Gracie openly listened and empathized. That level of communication didn't fix the class dynamic (that was on Mrs. Perez), but it kept their friendship intact. And that's a win.

Reflection

- When others give us hard evidence that they cannot be trusted, we should not ignore it. What are clues that a person is not trustworthy?

- Think of a time when you made an assumption about someone else's motives. How did that complicate the relationship?

- How do you see cynicism permeating our culture? Seeping into your school? Your friend group? Yourself?

- Do you consider yourself easy to read or cryptic? Why? How does that transparency either help or hurt your friendships?

SCENE 4

Indirect vs. Direct Communication

B eing the class treasurer is a thankless job, Caleb concludes after just one month in the role. The class president basks in the spotlight, the VP and secretary have all the social connections and take credit for all of *his* work, and the two faculty sponsors are so busy and preoccupied that they can't read the dynamics of this team. Often Caleb is left doing all the actual work solo. Caleb's initial annoyance morphs into irritation, which bubbles into anger, so he takes matters into his own hands.

When it's budget time, he runs his proposal past the more distracted faculty sponsor. She's an art teacher and probably hasn't looked at a spreadsheet in eons, so he knows she will unquestioningly approve whatever ideas he submits, as long as he does not overspend their budget.

When the students complain about the class president's narcissistic style, Caleb doesn't even have to chime in. They can tell he's a sympathetic listener, so they start coming directly to him with their ideas and questions and circumvent the president. In no time flat, he has become the go-to person on the student council. When the president speaks, Caleb doesn't contradict him directly, but his silence and his skeptical expression communicate loudly. His classmates will for sure vote for him as president next year.

When the sponsors ask the leaders how things are going, Caleb hints at the underlying power struggle, but the sponsors are too distracted and the other leaders too self-absorbed to grasp his meaning, so he continues his stealth campaign to undermine the team. And it works.

(Side note: If you want to see this same power dynamic play out in a family, read the devastating true story of King David's conflict with his sons in 2 Samuel 13–19. What a mess! One rape, unpunished; led to one murder, unaddressed; led to one son in isolation, stewing; led to a bloody coup, brewing; led to a war, unleashed; led to thousands of soldiers' deaths, one more dead son, and a heartbroken father. You can't make this stuff up. King David could have avoided much of the pain and heartache by *communicating directly* with his boys. Did God still use him in His grand plan for humanity? Yes. But it didn't have to play out like this.)

An Unhealthy Team

Indirect communication is a key symptom of a toxic environment. What can that look like?

> Going around the person you really should talk to. (If you have a problem with your coach, talk to him—not to the trainer or assistant coach, hoping he or she will sort it out for you.)
> Gossiping about someone, rather than talking directly with the person about the problem or potential solutions. (If you have a problem with friend A, do not talk about your issue with friend B. Go straight to friend A.)
> Asking permission from the person you believe is most likely to say yes. (Don't avoid your strict/cautious parent and gravitate toward your relaxed/permissive parent.)
> Hinting at the real message without saying what you really mean. (If you're not "fine," then don't tell your friends and/

or family you're "fine" and expect them to read between the lines.)

Telling someone else to communicate a message for you, instead of telling the ultimate recipient yourself. (If you're going to miss rehearsal, tell the director yourself; don't ask your friend to pass along that message for you.)

Giving a "softer" message than the actual content that needs to be communicated, hoping the recipient will read between the lines. (If your mom embarrassed you, then you don't have to crucify her, but you can find a way to gently, clearly tell her how you feel.)

Using nonverbal cues or sarcasm to communicate a different meaning than your words. (Tempting, but just don't.)

The Consequences

The choices we make between interacting directly or indirectly with others are not just personal preferences or personality styles. The consequences of indirect communication have a real-life negative impact on our relationships with others:

- Undermined trust
- Multiplied miscommunication
- Growing conflict and resentment
- Clouds of confusion
- People taking "sides," which undermines team cohesion
- The source of the problem growing foggy, making it harder to solve

Necessary? No! Preventable? Yes! The obvious remedy? Direct communication.

A Better Way

Most of us theoretically agree that communicating directly is good/wise/healthy. But many of us do not actually follow this process. Let's look at some timeless truth, courtesy of the Master Teacher:

> "If your brother or sister sins, go and point out their fault, just between the two of you. If they listen to you, you have won them over. But if they will not listen, take one or two others along, so that 'every matter may be established by the testimony of two or three witnesses.' If they still refuse to listen, tell it to the church; and if they refuse to listen even to the church, treat them as you would a pagan or a tax collector." (Matthew 18:15–17 NIV)

Notice what Jesus did *not* say: "If your friend hurts your feelings, first, give her the silent treatment. Stop talking to her. Act as if she doesn't exist. Second, aim for social isolation. Don't comment on or like her posts. Make her feel excluded. Don't invite her to anything. Third, talk about her behind her back. Gossip, slander, backstab. Make her pay for what she did to you. Then, and only then, will you feel satisfied." That method can be tempting, and we have probably all been on the receiving end of that malicious approach. But in the end, nothing good comes of it: no resolution, no actual happiness, and no peace.

Notice what Jesus *did* tell us to do. When your friend sins against you, go directly to her first. Tell her what happened and how it made you feel. Articulate your feelings and then listen: She might have something to add to the conversation, whether it's an apology or just some context. If you had a part in the conflict, then own it and apologize. If your friend won't listen to you, then take one other mutual friend, someone with a cool head who has a reputation for making peace, not for stirring up more drama. If that still doesn't work, then involve a trusted adult, such as a coach, adviser, or school counselor who knows you both and wants what's best for you both. For the 1 percent of friendships that are still in turmoil after following this process, give it some grace and space. Grace + space works miracles; gossip + slander hurts you both.

Is Jesus' method easy? No, it's easier to gossip. Direct confrontation can feel uncomfortable. But Jesus' way is always best, and ultimately, it's easier to put out a small brush fire than to hose down an entire forest.

One vital caveat: If there's a power imbalance in the relationship, then take someone else with you, i.e., if you have a conflict with a teacher/coach/leader who has direct authority over you and the potential to make your life miserable, then you may need to take a parent or advocate (such as an assistant coach or other teacher) with you to help facilitate the conversation. If you aren't sure how to read those dynamics, talk to your parents first. That's not gossip; that's God's built-in system to protect minors.

Parallel Universe

What if Caleb, the class treasurer we mentioned, had employed direct communication instead of initiating his campaign of sabotage? What if at the next leadership meeting, he had expressed how he felt in a mature way, not attacking his team but expressing his legitimate frustrations in a healthy way? What if he had pulled the president aside and asked for help? What if he had met with the two faculty sponsors and asked them to actually review his budget? What if he had employed direct communication rather than undermined the entire student council with his indirect communication? Well, in that parallel universe, if Caleb had chosen the better way, then the student leaders would have rallied together, formed a close working alliance, and led a series of incredible projects for their class that year. Caleb would have proudly listed "class treasurer" on his college applications and used the skills he learned from that experience in his future accounting job. In that parallel universe, the ripples of his good choices just keep going.

Reflection

- Which types of indirect communication do you observe in your circles (classes, teams in school/work/sports/clubs/arts, friend circles, etc.)?

- Which type bothers you the most? Why do you think that is?

- Which type of indirect communication do you occasionally revert to? Why is that your negative default?

- Think back to a recent conflict with a friend, sibling, teammate, or family member. How could you apply the Matthew 18 concepts to that situation? How might that have dampened the fire before it exploded?

SCENE 5

Emotional Intelligence

Austin comes from a big family: two parents, five kids, three dogs, a turtle, two fish, and a guinea pig with a gift for disappearing. His house often feels like swirling chaos and a vicious competition for the last piece of pizza. In birth order, Austin falls second. His older brother, Alex, is a certified genius, the disgusting kind who earns A's without trying, maxes out his AP class options, and even takes a course in the summer so he can fit in more classes during the school year. Alex casts a big shadow. Austin is smart, but he doesn't feel like it. He earns solid B's and a few low A's, but he doesn't live for school the way Alex does. In his honest moments, Austin admits to himself that he feels inferior to Alex.

One catch, though, and this is what Austin can't clearly see yet: Austin is great with people, while Alex is socially awkward, which is putting it mildly. Austin walks into school and knows everyone. He's friendly and comfortable in his own skin and can have actual conversations with his teachers, looking them in the eye and connecting with them. He's charming. Awkward Alex averts his eyes, speaks quietly, and kind of inches away from the person he's speaking to.

In other words, Austin has high emotional intelligence, while Alex has low emotional intelligence. In a traditional school setting, Alex "wins": he wins the academic prizes, the race for valedictorian, the killer test scores. But as soon as they launch past school, Austin will effortlessly outshine his brother. As soon as clients and employers no longer care about their unweighted GPA or ACT scores, what they will care about is whether they can call Austin when they have a problem, whether he'll listen to them, whether he'll empathize with them, and whether he feels like their go-to person who gets them. That's a gift.

The Gift of Empathy

One of the more common and dangerous human assumptions is that everyone views the world the same way we do. Each of us tends to default to that logic. We look at a situation and see X, so we assume that everyone else must see an identical image.

But what about the student who sits next to you who grew up in Brazil and just moved to the States two years ago?

What about the student who lives out on a farm, surrounded by open space and natural beauty, rather than concrete suburbia?

What about the student who splits his time between his mom's flat and his dad's condo?

What about the student whose grandparents are raising her?

What about the student who's Muslim? Who's Jewish? Who's atheist? Who's Christian?

What about the student whose mom is a state Supreme Court justice?

What about the student whose dad is applying for citizenship and lives with the haunting fear that his dad will be deported before it comes through?

What about the student who has moved seventeen times in the past decade because of her parent's job?

What about the student wearing brand new Golden Goose shoes to school vs. the student who's worrying about how her parents are going to make rent?

You get it. We are all shaped by our unique and varied experiences.

Some of those differences are highly visible to the naked eye, but many nuances are hidden, deeply buried, but influential. We may assume that others view the world the same way we do, but the reality is that each of us has a lens through which we see life. Your lens is unique, and so is mine.

My Lens

Seeing life through my particular lens warps my vision. I might experience the same event you do, but I focus on something very different in the experience. I see, understand, synthesize, and respond to that event in my way, while you respond to the exact same event in your way. Neither is right or wrong; neither is 100 percent pure or objective. We are both influenced by our prior knowledge, deep-seated beliefs about life, and our own self-interest.

Consider the case of the camp counselors. Sophia and Leo are both counselors at Sun & Sky Day Camp for elementary students. They're both natural with kids: patient, high-energy, and fun. But during their staff training in June, Sophia felt inspired, while Leo felt frustrated.

See, Sophia grew up going to this very same camp. Some of her happiest memories as a kid are those weeks at Sun & Sky, making new friends, going down the water slide, learning archery, creating messy crafts, and doing structured games out in the North Carolina sunshine. When Sophia hears the camp director skimming through the rules, she hardly listens; she can't wait to be assigned her group of campers, and she is imagining reliving her own experience as a kid.

Leo, on the other hand, grew up going to Pine Ridge in Tennessee, where he went rafting and basically lived and played outdoors, free range, for two weeks. Pine Ridge had few rules and max freedom. So when he hears the camp director drilling all these restrictive rules, he rolls his eyes. From his perspective, how can kids explore the natural world with so little freedom?

The camp director, Eden, is emphasizing the safety rules hard this year. A friend of hers runs a camp in the Northeast and had two terrible accidents with her campers last session. Eden is, understandably, terrified. Yes, she wants her campers to have fun, but the baseline expectation is that she keep these kids safe and return them to their parents intact. Happy is a bonus; safe is a requirement.

Sophia, Leo, and Eden are all living the same moment, but they could not experience it more differently.

People Skills

Understanding someone else's perspective is not just a cognitive process but also includes the ability to read another person's emotional state through facial expressions, body language, gestures, tone of voice, and eyes. Research shows that humans perceive and decode these nonverbal cues far more quickly than we can process a person's words, which means that we tend to react more to what we perceive (nonverbal) than to what we hear (verbal)—which also means that it's vitally important that we are reading nonverbal cues correctly. Some people are innately good at this. Some of us have to work at it.

Wyatt's dad is crazy good at this. Wyatt knows that people love his dad. There's something about him, some charisma or magic or warmth that draws people to him. He's semi–book smart, or at least clever enough to have started his own home hospice care company a decade ago, but conventional intelligence isn't the key to his success. He can read people. He walks into a room and feels the energy of the crowd. Without even trying, he can set someone at ease in a conversation. Whether they're with clients in the suite at Soldier Field for a Bears game or at an awards ceremony at Wyatt's school, everyone seems to know his dad, and somehow, his dad makes everyone he talks to feel special and important. He's off-the-charts people smart. Wyatt doesn't feel that same confidence with people, but he's studying his dad. *Maybe at age sixteen Dad hadn't learned his magic yet; maybe I can grow into it*, Wyatt hopes.

Empathy Gap

Humans aren't born with an empathy gene. If you spend any time with little kids (like younger siblings, babysitting charges), then you know that children are not innately empathetic. Empathy is a learned skill. Share your toys? Stop playing because someone fell off the slide? Let someone else eat the last popsicle? Watch a friend's requested show instead of your favorite episode of *Bluey*? No, no, no, no!

These self-centered instincts don't erode with time. The empathy gap has become a full gulf in our culture. As parenting has become child-centered and education has become student-centered, we teach children to focus primarily on themselves by asking them, "What would *you* like to do? What do *you* want? What makes *you* happy? What would *you* like to learn?" Parents can include their children in decisions without surrendering to them as dictators. Sometimes kids don't want to eat broccoli, get enough sleep, or limit their screen time, but wise parents choose what's best for their children, not what makes them happy in the moment. In the long run, those kids who have been catered to their whole lives grow into entitled teens and adults. The tantrum toddler morphs into the tyrant teen, and let's be honest—that person is unbearable.

Empathy requires maturity and imagination. We shift our perspective from "me" to "we," and we see life through others' eyes. We make decisions that factor other people in, e.g., "If I choose this, then how does that affect my family?"

Max learned the importance of empathy thanks to his mom. His dream has been to play soccer for an MLS academy. The catch: The team that has shown interest in him is in Colorado, and he and his family live in Atlanta. At first Max was so fixated on fulfilling his dream, for which he has worked incredibly hard, that he was willing to sacrifice anything for it. Some of the players on the team live with host families, or they move with one parent to Colorado while the other stays home with the other kids.

At first Max could only filter this decision through his own lens, but he started to broaden his view. He could sense the pain his mom felt over tearing their family in half. His two younger sisters are thriving in their school and in their track club in Atlanta. Slowly Max realized that this decision was much bigger than he'd initially thought. His empathy does not mean that he can't move to Colorado, but it does mean that he can recognize that this is a family decision. He's affecting five lives, not one. Once Max acknowledged the complexity of the decision, his mom actually grew more open-minded, because she saw that Max had the maturity to process the toll on the whole family and wasn't just thinking about himself.

Is there a right or wrong decision here? Not necessarily. But the empathy at the core of Max's experience is absolutely right.

Reality Check

Empathy isn't a by-product of age. Some adults, even leaders and seasoned people in positions of authority, have a major blind spot: They cannot see from another's perspective. We want to shake them and remind them that . . .

1. You are not the center of the universe.
2. Your personal preferences aren't the sole factor in decisions.
3. Others think/see/feel differently than you do—and that's okay!
4. You need to work to understand others, just as you want them to work to understand you.
5. Effective communicators speak the language of their listeners; they don't expect others to cater to their style.

Can we all learn or sharpen those social-emotional skills? Absolutely. Even pathological narcissists can change, if they choose to.

Multiply Your EI Quota

In addition to all the social-emotional assembly speakers you hear at school and the books you read for that psychology elective class and the reminders your mom has hammered into your brain whenever she dropped you off at a friend's house, let's focus on those basic human connection skills:

> **Listen well.** Use active listening to check for understanding of what the speaker is sharing.
>
> **Observe carefully.** Notice people's little tics and reactions. Why did that person betray a whiff of frustration? How does she view this tension? Watch without judgment.
>
> **Cultivate personal relationships.** Spend time with people on their turf. That friend loves movies? Go see one together. Your sibling loves to shop for cologne? Tag along.
>
> **Show curiosity.** People love to talk about themselves. Give others a chance. Ask questions and give them the gift of your listening. How rare to discover someone who actually listens to and cares about what we say—and how intoxicating.

Reflection

- Think of someone you know with high emotional intelligence. How quickly can he or she read the room? Why do you think he or she is so good with people? Is that a born gift or a honed skill?

- What makes someone easy to talk to?

- Empathy comes with maturity, not age. How have you grown in your ability to empathize with others? As you look back, can you see growth in your ability to really listen to others who are different from you and see life through their eyes?

- Have you noticed the trend in our culture of a growing lack of empathy? Describe.

- Think of someone in your life you find challenging. How can seeing life through his or her eyes help your relationship?

Act 2

MANAGING ANGER

SCENE 1

Overwhelming Emotions

D o you ever feel like the Hulk, or do you know anyone with temper issues like his? Mild-mannered fictional physicist Dr. Bruce Banner explodes into a green monster of unleashed rage. Banner fights the world, and he also fights against himself. When his friend Black Widow quizzes him on his secret of self-control, his ability to cling to his human form and avoid "the other guy," Banner eventually explains, "That's my secret, I'm always angry."

Ever feel like that?

Aristotle observed, "Anyone can become angry—that is easy, but to be angry with the right person at the right time, and for the right purpose and in the right way—that is not within everyone's power, and that is not easy." Amen? *Amen*.

Infectious Anger

Anger is a powerful and misunderstood emotion. We see/feel/experience it everywhere. Angry parents. Angry teachers. Angry students. Angry coaches. Angry voters. Angry drivers. Angry siblings. Angry friends. They rage at us, and we rage right back.

Have you ever been in the airport when a flight is canceled? That's a scene of mass outrage.

Have you ever watched a parent whose talented son got no playing time in a big game? A lava-spewing Mount Vesuvius would be safer.

Have you ever known someone consumed with anger at himself or herself? That's a particularly sticky wrath to escape.

But can anger ever be good, positive, and healthy?

Does anger serve any productive purpose?

When we feel anger, how do we constructively respond? Repressing it only leads to a volcanic eruption, so what should we do when the green rage possesses us?

What Is Anger?

Although we often label *anger* as a singular emotion, the reality is that anger is a cluster of emotions that involve the body, the mind, and the will. Anger is not a cold, calculated choice. No one calmly decides, "I think I will feel angry now." That sounds absurd, doesn't it? Anger is an involuntary reaction to irritation, frustration, embarrassment, pain, fear, or sadness.

Thousands of things might trigger our anger: Great-Aunt Alice makes a tactless comment about your little sister's weight. The reckless blue Audi on the highway tails you way too closely. Your volatile dad always seems ready to lose his temper, and you seem to have inherited the trait. Your ex-best friend is now talking to your ex-boyfriend. See the injustice ⤍ trigger the anger. Anger pits us directly against the person or event that harmed us.

Even God gets angry. Oh yes, when God sees evil or injustice, He feels anger. Fortunately, God is "slow to anger" (see Numbers 14:18), but when He sees something horribly wrong, He feels angry. Our anger toward injustice mimics His because we're made in His image, yet His anger is pure and devoid of selfish motives, and He never loses His temper. His reaction is always perfectly measured and perfectly balanced between His holiness (His unimpeachable purity) and His love (the strongest force in the universe). God never betrays His holiness, and He never betrays His love.

Want to see proof of God's anger? When His anger burned against His faithless people on the cusp of conquest, He made them wander in the wilderness for forty years (see Numbers 32:13). When Jesus saw greedy merchants gouging innocent people in His temple, He flipped their benches over and cleaned house (see Matthew 21:12–13). These are two examples of righteous anger: sinless and laser-focused on restoring what's right.

Anger is not evil. It's not sinful. It's not part of our fallen nature. It's not evidence of the enemy's work in our lives. Quite the contrary. Anger is evidence that we are made in God's image. Our anger proves that we, despite being fallen and broken and imperfect humans living in a fallen and broken and imperfect world, still have a deep, innate concern for justice, fairness, and rightness. Our capacity for anger proves that we are more than mere animals. Our anger is evidence of our nobility, not of our depravity.

A Mark of Maturity

The ability to sift through our emotions is a sign of maturity. Children are often overwhelmed by their emotions. They go from zero to one hundred in no time flat. Are they crying because they're hungry, sleepy, lonely, sad, hurting, scared, _____? Honestly, the child may not know, so when you watch a savvy parent in action, you see that parent triage very quickly what her child's real problem is. She may feed her son a quick snack while simultaneously scanning for injury and looking at his sleepy eyes and feeling his forehead and giving him a reassuring hug and listening to the exact tone of his cries. That mom is a skilled lion tamer.

The lion grows up and starts to self-regulate. By middle and high school, many students have developed healthy survival skills, but then hormones kick in. The swirl of hormones in puberty can tip the equilibrium of even the most stable human. That's normal. When we feel a rush of overwhelming emotions, which happens to everyone, we have to step back and ask ourselves, "What exactly am I feeling, and why?" The ability to articulate our own emotions and sift through their causes is a clear mark of maturity. Sometimes we feel as if the whole world is ending, but it's just a semi-bad day amplified by hormones and/or sleep deprivation and/or eating junk. The mature teen can sift through all that. "Yes, it *feels* like the end of the world, but in reality, this is just a normal-size problem. I feel off today."

The correct response may not be the nuclear option (break up with my boyfriend, quit my job, cancel all my closest friends, lose my temper on my clueless but sincere mom). The correct response might be more along the lines of drinking 32 ounces of water, eating a vegetable or twelve, sleeping for eight straight hours, and then starting fresh tomorrow. You might roll your eyes at how stupid and mundane that sounds, but deep down you know it's true.

Remember the last time you felt angry? Now dig for the *why*. We can all think of a situation. Once we sift past all the extenuating circumstances (hormones, sleep deprivation, stress over a calculus test), our anger is likely tied to a sense of injustice. Our anger can be directed toward another person, a circumstance, God, or even ourselves, but in each case, we feel as if someone treated us wrongly. When we perceive that our parents are being unfair and unreasonable, we feel angry. When we see bullies target innocent victims, we feel angry. When we watch our teachers grind us mercilessly on deadlines but then take three months to grade our essays, we feel angry. "That's not right," we grumble to ourselves. True. It's not right.

The Magic Question

But what do we do with our anger? Ah, the magic question. It's easy to spot wrong responses to anger (e.g., violence, vengeance, or verbal vitriol). How should we channel our anger in a productive way?

Human anger is designed by God to motivate us to take constructive action in the face of wrongdoing or injustice. In God's design, we channel our anger into motivation for taking positive, loving actions; setting wrongs right; and restoring broken relationships. Anger does not give us blanket license to say or do destructive things to others, even if they were wrong. After the dust settles, our anger should motivate us to leave situations and people better than when we found them, not to leave a trail of broken bodies and bruised souls in our wake.

Anger is like that glaring red "check engine" light flashing in the car, indicating that a problem needs attention. Anger can be a powerful and positive motivator to move us toward loving action to right wrongs and correct injustice—but it can also become a raging, uncontrolled force. Anger isn't wrong, but how we respond to it can be.

Mirror, Mirror

Our anger actually reflects our hearts. Tell me what you are angry about, and I will tell you what is most important to you.

If you're most heated because of some cruel, critical words you found out one of your friends said about you, then I know how much you value friendship and loyalty.

If you're furious over how your mom was unceremoniously fired without cause, or about how your brother's coach made him feel worthless, then I know how highly you value and want to protect your family.

If you can't get over how someone created a deepfake video of you, then I know you do your best to guard your reputation.

If you are fixated on the teacher at your school whose life mission is to lower your GPA, then I know you're invested in your academic success and expect fairness from authorities.

If you keep dwelling on how a fellow student was wrongly suspended from school for something he didn't even do, then clearly you value justice.

If you watch and rewatch that video contrasting celebrity excess with starving children, then you are motivated by compassion and equity. You get the point. What fires you up reveals who you are. As we mature, ideally our anger will focus *more* on true injustice and unfairness and *less* on petty personal irritations. As we mature, our anger will convert into energy to try to make the world a better, more just, more beautiful place. As we mature, our anger will also be tempered by humility, that sense of our own brokenness, rather than fueled by self-righteous hypocrisy.

A mature person has the potential to understand and process anger in a healthy way, knowing that the world doesn't revolve around me and that I can live with a genuine sense of gratitude for all I have been given.

Reflection

- Many of us subconsciously think that anger is bad, so we're tempted to ignore or suppress anger. In your mind, is anger innately good or bad? What's behind your answer?

- Describe a time when you felt overwhelmed by your own emotions. As you look back now, how do you sift through what was going on in your own mind, soul, and body—which are all closely linked?

- In your own experience, what are some wrong responses to anger? What are some constructive responses to anger?

- Sometimes we get angry when someone does to us the very things we do to others. This is an ancient but true concept: "Do not pay attention to every word people say, or you may hear your servant cursing you—for you know in your heart that many times you yourself have cursed others" (Ecclesiastes 7:21–22 NIV). How can you apply this principle in your life?

- What does your anger reveal about you? Consider the things that infuriate you; what does each of those targets show about your values and heart?

SCENE 2

Valid vs. Invalid Anger

Ava got a message from a girl she doesn't know . . . with unsavory details about her own boyfriend, Carter. Carter, apparently, had been sending very personal messages to this other girl. When that girl found out that Carter already had a girlfriend—in fact, a long-term relationship as he and Ava had been together for eighteen months, the girl stopped talking to Carter and sent a message to Ava. "I thought you should know," the girl wrote.

Ava was devastated. She had thought their relationship was unshakable. She'd dreamed that even when they went off to college, they'd stay together. She had been through so much with Carter and had been a constant support to him during his parents' drawn-out divorce.

Her dominant emotion is sadness, but triggered by that sadness is a deep, simmering anger. And rightly so—this is valid anger. Carter blindsided and betrayed Ava. How he treated her was wrong. No matter what is going on in his life, she doesn't deserve that.

Last week Charlotte couldn't find her hoodie. She tried not to assume the worst of her sister, but Chloe was guilty as charged. Hoodie borrowed, hoodie lost. Chloe is so loose with things that it didn't even register with her that Charlotte would care. She brushed it off. "You have another gray hoodie," Chloe said casually.

That was a hoodie. This evening when Charlotte strolled into the garage, ready to drive to volleyball practice, she came to an abrupt halt. Her car was gone. She checked her sister's location: the mall. A frantic text string ensued. Yes, Chloe had her car. "I didn't think you'd care," Chloe wrote. "Be home soon." Her version of "soon" might be fifteen minutes or two hours; either way Charlotte will be late to practice.

What does Charlotte feel? Anger. Valid anger.

Anger falls into two camps: valid and invalid. Let's visit each of those camps.

Processing Valid Anger

Valid anger is provoked by *genuine wrongdoing* on the part of the other person. When we feel valid anger, we should (loosely) follow four simple steps:

1. Acknowledge your anger.
2. Pause your immediate, gut-check response.
3. Laser-focus on the source of your anger.
4. Analyze your options and choose a constructive response.

One step at a time now . . .

Step 1: Acknowledge your anger.

That might sound so obvious that you're rolling your eyes. "Of course I'm angry!" you might snap.

But some people are blindsided by their own anger, which hits them like a tsunami. Swept away, they lash out, and they never stop to register why. Their response precedes any conscious choice or thought.

Rather than being baffled by and then swept away by your anger, acknowledge aloud, or at least in your mind, that you *are* angry and *why* you are angry. Then, and only then, will you be in a position to make a conscious choice about your response. Lead with reason, not emotion.

Step 2: Pause your immediate, gut-check response.

What's your immediate response when you feel that wave of anger? Yeah, whatever that is, don't do that.

Few adults have ever learned how to channel their anger. Most of us unconsciously follow the patterns we saw growing up, which tend to cluster around the two extremes: either fiery verbal/physical venting or icy withdrawal and silence. Both responses tend to be destructive. We have to unlearn those bad habits and relearn healthy habits. This doesn't mean we suppress our anger and pretend everything is fine. Rather, we refuse to let the monster take over. Consider the proverb, "Fools give full vent to their rage, but the wise bring calm in the end" (Proverbs 29:11 NIV). Don't be that guy, that fool who's spewing his rage on everyone in proximity to him. Can you think of a time you did that? Most of us can. In the immediate flush of anger, we say horrible things we later regret—and we can never erase those words.

"I can't control my anger," you might argue. False. You can control your anger. Once the lava starts spewing, then it's difficult to turn off the flow, but there's always a moment of decision, just before the volcano erupts, when you choose self-control or self-indulgence. In that moment, pause. Two strategies that help people I talk with are to either count to ten (or to one hundred, if needed) or to walk away. This does not mean you're pausing your response for three months or indefinitely, but it does mean you give yourself the five minutes you need so that you can control your emotions, not let them control you.

Step 3: Laser-focus on the source of your anger.

Why are you actually angry? We've discussed this step before, but it's a pivotal moment in your response.

When your history teacher hands back your graded research paper with a glaring C+ on the top, are you angry at her for being too tough of a grader? (Seriously, she should teach college.) Or are you angry at your dad for putting too much pressure on you? He has such unrealistic expectations. Or are you mad at yourself for waiting till the night before to write your essay, when you also had math homework and a playoff game? Or is it some combination of the three? In your moment of pause (step 2), focus: Who am I actually angry with, and why?

And how serious is the matter? Was that paper worth 50 percent of your semester grade in a showcase class, or will it have minimal effect on your GPA?

Or when your mom is late to pick you up, is that an innocent mistake because she's frantically doing so much for your family, or did she leave you stranded somewhere for hours and completely forget about you for the seventh time?

Focus.

Step 4: Analyze your options and choose a constructive response.
How should you respond to an offense? With a verbal lashing? Character assassination? Social media war? Act as if the person is dead to you? An eye for an eye? Public humiliation? Personal attack? The options are limitless.

But there are really only two good options: either let it go or confront the offender.

The let-it-go option: In the minority of cases, I acknowledge that I'm angry, I pause and diagnose the *who* and the *why*, and I realize that confronting the person holds zero redemptive value for the offender or for me. So I let it go and roll it off to God. This is not the same as stuffing or suppressing my anger. It is quite the opposite. It is releasing the anger to God. It is giving up my right to take revenge, which is actually not my right; it's God's (see Romans 12:19). It's refusing to let what happened to me in the past eat away at me in the present or in the future. It's a conscious choice to release the offense and move on. It's my confidence that God is perfectly just, He is totally aware of my situation, and He will make all things right in the end. But not yet. Until then, I refuse to be an emotional captive to the wrongdoing or the wrongdoer.

Sometimes this is the best option. For example, let's say your grandfather has always cruelly compared you to your cousin. When you were younger, if you scored ten points in your basketball game, he'd say, "Oh, you think that's impressive? Liam scored twenty points, and he's the team MVP." When you were in middle school, he accused you of being short and weak. Once you hit your growth spurt, he said you looked too tall, and then he slipped in a comment about Liam's perfect height. You got good grades? Liam's were better. It was almost comical, except that it was pointed and hurtful and personal. In all those formative years when you could have used some unconditional support, he failed you.

Should you confront him? Well, now he has advanced dementia. Most days he can't tell you and Liam apart. What good would it do for you or for him to have that conversation? You choose to let it go and roll it off to God. In this case, that's the better option.

The confrontation option: In the majority of cases, though, the wise response to valid anger is to lovingly, directly confront the person who wronged you and to seek restitution. Back in Act 1, Scene 4, we explored this concept of confrontation. It's simple but also terribly hard. Jesus gave us the blueprint: "If your brother or sister sins, go and point out their fault, just between the two of you. If they listen to you, you have won them over" (Matthew 18:15 NIV). Step 1 is to go talk directly to the person. Notice that this advice applies to people with whom you have a close relationship—not to your state's governor whose education policy you dislike or to a famous influencer whose words offend you. When your friend/sibling/parent/coach/fellow cast member/etc. hurts you personally, you go talk to that individual personally. You bring the issue to his or her attention in a loving, direct style. This isn't verbal abuse; it's a *conversation*, and there's always a possibility that you misunderstood or misconstrued the person's words or actions, so listen carefully to the response. In this context of open communication, confrontation may lead to resolution: open air, free forgiveness, and genuine healing.

But if the person refuses to listen? Step 2: Take a mutual, calm friend or trusted mentor (Matthew 18:16) to facilitate the conversation.

But if the person still refuses to listen? Step 3: Distance! That is not a safe person for you to be near (Matthew 18:17).

The ideal formula is that loving confrontation leads to a restored relationship, but you can only control one variable in that equation: your own response.

Letting Go of Invalid Anger

Let's see if we can spot the difference between valid and invalid anger.

Camp 1: Someone lies about my character, steals my property, treats me like I'm subhuman, or hurts me personally. This type of anger is a reaction to wrongdoing or injustice. Valid or invalid?

Camp 2: This anger is triggered by a disappointment, an unfulfilled desire, a sense of frustration, an inconvenience, a bad mood, extreme stress or exhaustion, or any mix of other factors. Sure, the annoyance made my life trickier and triggered one of my emotional sensitivities, but it wasn't morally wrong. Valid or invalid?

Did you label camp 1 valid and camp 2 invalid? Well done. If we treat all anger as equally valid, then we will make some serious blunders in our responses.

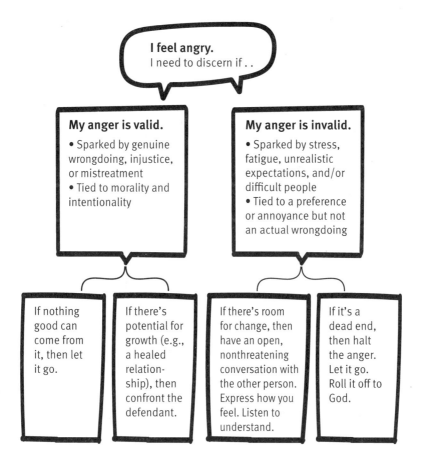

Sanity Check

Life doesn't always fit into a flow chart, and sometimes the lines between valid and invalid anger get muddied. In those times, who's your go-to person who will calmly look at the facts with you and then tell you the truth?

Daniela's person is Brie. See, Daniela can be fiery. She feels things deeply. She has a super-sensitivity toward life. Her highs are high, and her lows are low. She and Brie became friends years ago, so they've done some miles together. Brie knows and loves Daniela exactly as she is, but she can also calm Daniela down when needed. So when Daniela's anger spikes, she will say to Brie, "Sanity check?" She rattles off what happened, Brie listens, and then Brie weighs it in the grand scheme of life. "Yeah, that's ridiculous. I can see why you're mad," she sometimes says, but other times she says, "I know it's annoying, but let that one go." And Daniela is wise enough to listen to her person.

Reflection

- From your own life, brainstorm a time you felt valid anger about a genuine wrongdoing and brainstorm a time you felt invalid anger about an annoyance. How can you discern the difference?

- Look back over the four steps for processing valid anger. Where does your train tend to derail?

- That Matthew 18 confrontation process is a brilliant blueprint for life. Even though confrontation can feel hard, what are the benefits to following this process?

- Who's your go-to, clear-headed, calm-as-a-cucumber, sanity-check person who helps you discern valid vs. invalid anger? (Side note: If you don't have that kind of friend yet, then you need to *find* that kind of calm, wise friend, and you also need to *be* that kind of friend.)

SCENE 3

Explosions + Implosions

School is stressful for Trey. What masochist dreamed up ninety-minute academic blocks? Horrible. And most of his teachers love to hear themselves yap, so they just lecture, droning on and on and . . . He fluctuates between restless, can't sit still, fidgety, "May-I-go-to-the-bathroom again?" energy and feeling comatose, eyes rolled back in his head, not absorbing a word in the classroom. Academic torture.

Then there's the social hierarchy. This school is so cliquey: Who are your friends, who are your ex-friends, how do you label yourself, what activities can you list on your college application, how rich are you, how connected are your parents, which girl are you talking to now? Social torture.

Even football has politics. You'd think the faster, stronger, more skilled player would get the playing time, but no; Trey has to fight for everything on this team. Athletic torture.

By the time practice ends at 6:00 p.m., Trey feels drained in every way. When he walks into his house, his little brother, Bryce, races to see him, bored and lonely from playing alone for the past two hours. And the moment he steps in the house, his mom is calling out instructions to him: "Put a load of laundry in. Where's your practice uniform? Trash day is tomorrow. Did you put the trash and recycling cans in the street? Wait, the kitchen recycling is full. How much homework do you have tonight? How was your day? Why aren't you talking? Grandpa said you didn't text him back today. Help Bryce with his math, would you? I don't remember fractions. I have so much left to do tonight." He gets that she's tired, but he feels as if he just fought a nine-hour battle.

Within ninety seconds, Trey loses his temper on both of them, and Bryce stares up at him with those big brown eyes. Yet another failure in his day.

Explosions

Many of us take out our anger on our safe people. All day long we hold it together out in the public arena, but when we come home, we let it all loose. While it's good to have a safe place where we know we're unconditionally loved (what a gift), it's not okay to spew our harsh words and feelings on those closest to us just because we know they won't leave us. Want to guess who are teens' two favorite targets for their rage? Not their coaches, not their boyfriends/girlfriends, not their friends, not their teammates, not their teachers. Not anyone who has something they really want, such as playing time, good grades, or social capital. Teens most often explode on (1) their moms and (2) their siblings.

Many of us have never learned to channel our anger productively. We may have seen unhealthy patterns from our parents. The mom who's a screamer. The dad who throws a plate of pasta at the wall. The mom who's a passive-aggressive queen of withdrawal. The dad who road rages.

Explosive anger is never constructive. It not only hurts the person at whom it is directed, but it also destroys the self-esteem of the person who loses control. In the heat of an angry explosion, people say things they later regret; and later, when they reflect on their cosmic meltdown, they cannot feel good about themselves. These explosions ultimately destroy relationships. The person on the receiving end loses respect for the person who's out of control and eventually just avoids that person.

A few decades ago, it became popular in certain psychological circles to encourage clients to release their anger through aggressive behaviors, as long as that aggression wasn't directed toward a person. "Angry at your girlfriend? Beat this pillow! Do a few rounds against a punching bag! Smash a golf ball as far as you can!" However, follow-up research showed that physical venting of anger through aggression didn't actually drain the anger but did make the person more likely to physically erupt in the future. Mission failed. Explosions are not mature or acceptable ways to handle our anger.

Implosions

An explosion blows something apart. Picture a bomb. This is an outward force of destruction.

An implosion is a violent inward collapse. Picture a building slated for demolition collapsing in on itself. Implosive anger is equally destructive but detonates in a different direction: inward. This happens to the person who chooses to hold anger inside.

Explosive anger is easy to spot: screaming, swearing, criticizing, condemning, raging, and physically lashing out. Implosive anger can be tricky to identify because it is, by definition, internal. A person's life literally crumbles around the detonations of internalized anger.

Some Christians who would deplore explosive anger don't grasp that implosive anger is just as destructive in the long run. Implosive anger begins with silence and is typically characterized by three symptoms: denial, withdrawal, and brooding.

Denial sounds like this: "I'm not angry." This response is especially tempting for those who were taught that anger is sinful. Have you ever heard one of these lines?

"I'm not angry; I'm just very frustrated."

"I'm not angry; I'm just upset."

"I'm not angry, but I am disappointed."

"I'm not angry. I just don't like it when people treat me this way."

All of those lines start with the same claim: "I'm not angry." Oh, really? False. The underlying condition is pure, old-fashioned anger. Denying anger does not make it vanish. Internalized anger will have its destructive effect on the body and psyche of the angry individual.

With implosive anger, withdrawal is the central strategy. This "silent treatment" of withdrawal and avoidance may last for a day or for years. As long as it continues, resentment and bitterness grow and fester.

Cue the passive-aggressive behaviors. On the outside, the person appears calm and stoic ("Nothing is bothering me. I'm fine."), but eventually anger seeps out through the cracks. Have you seen these passive-aggressive moves?

- Ignoring someone's messages
- "Forgetting" to invite someone to an event
- Making snide comments ("That play in the game was surprisingly effective, given your lack of speed." "You look extra tired today.")
- Responding with sarcasm
- Refusing to engage in conversation, leaving the other person mystified
- No longer liking someone's posts, a virtual form of social isolation

There are endless variations on passive-aggressive behaviors, but they're all hostile, mean, aggressive, and *indirect*. The person won't tell me that she's mad at me and why; she will simply show me through her behaviors. These behaviors don't help the person process the original anger. It's still there, underground, needing to be dealt with.

Implosive anger taken to an extreme can mean an implosion in the form of an emotional breakdown, depression, or even self-harm.

Anger was meant to be a visitor, never a permanent resident, in the human heart. When we experience anger—and all of us experience anger sometimes—we need to deal with it and move on, not get permanently stuck in it.

Defusing the Bomb

The Danger: Implosive Anger

Definition: Internalized anger that is never expressed

Triggers: Fear of confrontation and/or the belief that anger is wrong

Clues: Denial ("I'm not angry.") and/or withdrawal ("I'm not angry; I'm just disappointed, and I need space.")

Results: Stress, passive-aggressive behaviors, resentment, bitterness, hatred, and even self-harm or violence

How to Defuse: Admit your implosive tendencies to yourself. Ask for help from a trusted adult (parent, counselor, pastor, coach). Deal with your anger directly; don't let it detonate your life from within.

The Caveat

Our subject in this chapter is what to do with *your* anger: don't explode, don't implode, just deal with it.

However, what if you aren't the one with the anger problem? What if you live with someone who is taking his or her anger out on you either through explosions or implosions? For some teens, that's the reality of their home lives. And if that's you, then know that it's not your fault, it's not your job to fix it, and you need to ask for help today.

Not next Wednesday. Today. Reach out to the guidance counselor at your school or call your pastor or your grandfather or your wild, loving aunt or your swim coach or your [fill in the blank with the safe adult who pops into your mind] today. As a counselor, I've talked with many teens, and I know it's healthy to reach out for help. Find the person who will be there for you. You're not alone.

Reflection

- Do you personally tend more toward explosive anger or implosive anger? Why do you think that is?

- Which is more common in your family of origin?

- What are the dangers of explosions?

- What are the dangers of implosions?

- Students are masters of passive-aggressive behaviors. What are some that you have seen or experienced?

- What do you think this means? "Anger was meant to be a visitor, never a permanent resident, in the human heart." In what ways can anger be a helpful visitor? How do you know if it's taken up permanent residence in your heart?

- Who are your safe people on whom you might be tempted to take out your stress?

SCENE 4

Underground Anger

Some volcanoes are silent for years, gurgling burning lava under the surface until a spectacular moment of eruption.

Other volcanoes burp little rivers of that lava in mini-eruptions. Same burning lava—released in small quantities.

The deadliest volcano in modern history happened in 1815 in Indonesia, directly claiming more than 100,000 human lives, plus animals, crops, trees, and anything else in its path. But then it just kept killing, causing tsunamis and even global crop failure, widespread famine, and disease. That single eruption, historians believe, may have caused more than one million deaths.[*]

Sometimes major eruptions are preceded by small blasts of steam and ash.

Some of the most dangerous volcanoes lie dormant for hundreds of years.

So it is with human anger. Left to boil inside the soul, anger bubbles and burns the person from the inside. When little annoyances or minor issues set the person off, a burst of burning steam and ash jets out—a warning sign of the danger within that person. Left unresolved, that anger keeps boiling until finally, we have a Mount Tambora. Rivers of lava burn everyone in the vicinity. The fiery flow can't be turned off. Those closest to the person either get burned or

---

[*] Becky Little, "The Deadliest Volcanic Eruption in History," History.com, September 29, 2023, https://www.history.com/news/the-deadliest-volcanic-eruption-in-history.

they run for their lives. It's an ugly scene of destruction.

This is the story of a person with unresolved, underground anger.

Seething Inside

Scarlett's dad left two winters ago. She had seen warning signs. Her parents lived very separate lives. On a Saturday night, she might get Thai food with her mom and sister, and they'd watch a girly movie together, and her dad would take her little brother to a baseball game. No family vacations for a few years. Her dad was cordial to her, but he honestly didn't seem to know anything about her. Her boyfriend's name? What colleges she was interested in? How she was doing in tennis? Her favorite class in school, and which class she was barely passing? He couldn't answer any of those questions.

And then he left. Packed his bags and vanished one December day. Her mom probably told her too much, details she wanted to know but also dreaded knowing, like how he had cheated on her mom back in Oregon and how they'd moved to California hoping for a fresh start. How her dad was controlling about her mom's spending, and the worse he treated her, the more she spent, like some manic cycle they couldn't seem to break.

That was two years ago. Scarlett watched her dad leave and then cut him completely out of her life. Blocked his number, refused to see him, pretended he didn't exist. Which, she argued to herself, he deserved, and which, she believed, was a way of protecting herself. But which, she also knew in her heart of hearts, did not help her move forward in her life. She was stuck back in that December day, two winters ago, watching him walk away.

And so the anger simmered and boiled and burned inside of her. For 99 percent of the time, she functioned beautifully. From the outside, it looked as if she had her life together. But inside, she was in turmoil, and it was only a matter of time before she erupted.

Signs of Underground Anger

You see, unresolved, underground anger doesn't just go away with time. It festers. In fact, that stored anger, over time, often leads to two outcomes: first, we can lash out at the people closest to us for little things; and second, we can become depressed.

Have you ever done that—lashed out at the people closest to you, even though they're not really the ones who wronged you? I have. Guilty as charged. We might be seething inside over a truly major injustice done to us. A coach shows favoritism, for example, and strands you on JV for a full year yet makes her daughter's best friend, who's not as talented as you, a varsity starter. Or a parent deserts you and starts over with a younger spouse and builds a new family. Or your dad is forced to take the blame at work over his team's bad investment, and suddenly your family income drops to zero.

Those are genuine injustices, and if you experienced one of those, you would feel righteous anger. But rather than dealing with the actual injustice, you might try to ignore it, and then when a hapless sophomore accidentally parks in your assigned spot at school, making you late to class, you react as if it's the end of the world. You don't really care about the parking spot. Sure, it's a minor annoyance, but it's not a real injury and it sure isn't personal. But the lava boiling over the true injustice spews out on the sophomore who just started driving to school (that poor, wide-eyed sophomore) and on everyone else who happens to be standing in the vicinity.

Whenever we are wronged, anger is the natural emotion that arises within us. The healthy way of addressing that anger is to directly and lovingly confront the person who wronged us and to work through it together, seeking resolution. Often, however, because of factors outside our control, we can't work through it. For example, kids seldom process their anger toward their parents because there's such a power imbalance in that relationship. The kids may fear their parents won't understand, or they fear that trying to address the issue will only make it worse. Therefore, they avoid confronting their parents, but the anger is still there. Wrongs are not forgotten unless they are processed. So we might complain about all the little annoyances in our lives and critically pick at all the people in closest proximity to us without ever actually dealing with the one issue and the one person who deeply hurt us.

Over time, if we have experienced a series of wrongs, our emotional ability to absorb those wrongs is stretched beyond capacity. Then the critical spirit sets in. And then often—not always, but often—the beginning stages of depression set in too.

Remember that anger serves a purpose: to motivate us to take constructive action with the person who wronged us. If we fail to do this, our unresolved anger heats up and becomes that boiling lava inside us, just waiting to spew little bits on the innocent people around us and scarring our own souls from within.

What can those opening stages of depression look like? When we feel we have been wronged, wronged, wronged throughout our lives, the heaviness of that injustice settles on our emotions. We might find ourselves becoming lethargic toward life, no longer interested in the things that used to spark joy for us. If we don't take steps to solve the real problem (the underground anger), then we can become more explosive or more depressed.

If that pattern resonates with you, then pause your reading and pick your trusted adult—a parent, guidance counselor, youth pastor, coach, or teacher—who can talk with you and connect you to a counselor who can help you work through the real issue: the underground anger. Asking for help is not a sign of weakness; it's a sign of maturity and self-awareness.

In my many years of counseling, I've seen almost everything under the sun. Some people manage to function well for a long time, untroubled by their underground anger. Sooner or later, though, something sets them off. That unprocessed anger will either burn the ones they love (through critical words, emotional distance, even physical violence) or burn them (through self-criticism, emotional detachment, even depression). I am *not* suggesting that all depression is caused by unresolved anger. That's false. I am telling you that depression is sometimes the symptom of a deeper problem of stored anger that has been boiling inside for years.

There's no magic, one-size-fits-all formula for addressing that underground anger. Sometimes we can personally confront the person who hurt us. Sometimes that's not wise or even possible. (More on that in Act 1, Scene 4 and in Act 2, Scene 2.) Hash that out through prayer and with a wise adult. When we pray, we can ask God very specific questions: "How should I deal with this wound? Do You want me to talk to the person who hurt me? Is it safe for me to do that? What do You want me to say?" When in doubt, ask Him! "If any of you lacks wisdom," wrote James, the half brother of Jesus, "you should ask God, who gives generously to all without finding fault, and it will be given to you" (James 1:5 NIV). And talk it all out with a safe adult (parent, pastor, counselor) who has your best interests at heart and who has seen enough of life to give you some wise input.

Homework

In the meantime, let me share a mini-project with you that has helped hundreds of my clients. All you need is a pencil, paper, and some alone time.

Reflect back over your life, and make a chart that answers two questions:

> *Who are the people who have hurt me?* Title this column "People."
> *What did they do to me?* Title this column "Pains."

People	Pains

Start with your childhood. Look at your early, formative relationships with your mom, dad, and siblings. If each of them wronged you at some point, which would be normal and expected, then list their names and the ways they wronged you. List specific details or memories. For example, if your brother shoved you off a climbing wall so you needed stitches, then write his name and exactly what he did to you when you were five years old.

Think about school. Did a teacher or student hurt you? Write the person's name and offense. The teacher who crushed your confidence? The student who socially isolated you? The coach who humiliated you? Write it all down.

Broaden your lens to look at any other relationships (friends, exes, people in your neighborhood or church or any other sphere). Every wound that comes to mind—write it down.

It's an interesting exercise to visually see the things we have held on to, sometimes for years. What we hold on to also holds on to us.

Revenge or Release?

It's understandable to want revenge. Think back to Scarlett's story at the beginning of the chapter: she intended to hurt her dad as much as he had hurt her.

But here's the truth, and I bet you already know this, even if you don't want to admit it. Revenge never satisfies us. Getting revenge will not fix the past, nor will it heal the wound in your heart, nor will it ever really balance the cosmic scales of justice. Think about the classic, savory revenge plots: *Hamlet*, *The Count of Monte Cristo*, *Murder on the Orient Express*, even *The Princess Bride*. ("My name is Inigo Montoya. You killed my father. Prepare to die.") Revenge can't heal the past, and it can't heal us.

There's a better way. It's hard, but it heals. The apostle Paul spells it out for us:

> Do not repay anyone evil for evil. Be careful to do what is right in the eyes of everyone. If it is possible, as far as it depends on you, live at peace with everyone. Do not take revenge, my dear friends, but leave room for God's wrath, for it is written: "It is mine to avenge; I will repay," says the Lord. On the contrary:
> "If your enemy is hungry, feed him;
> if he is thirsty, give him something to drink.
> In doing this, you will heap burning coals on his head."
> Do not be overcome by evil, but overcome evil with good. (Romans 12:17–21 NIV)

It is never our job to vindicate ourselves or to make people pay for the wrongs they did to us. God is the ultimate Judge, and He will make all things right in the end.

Go back to your list. Get alone with God. Read each name and each offense to God. Out loud! Then say, "You know what my dad did to me. You know how wrong that was and how much it hurt. You know how I've been carrying that inside me for all these years. Today I want to release him and how he hurt me to You. You are perfectly just and loving. You know everything about my dad. I don't know what motivated him to hurt me, but You know his motives and his actions. I choose to release him to Your justice." Reach your arm out toward God and imagine dropping a rock out of your hand into His hand. Let it go.

After you have prayed that over each line item on your list, ask God to teach you how to process your anger.

Finally, as a symbol of how you have released your pains to God, burn or shred the list. Don't set the house on fire, and don't leave that list lying around to remind you of the past.

Release it all to Him.

Review

Let's run that back one more time and review Scenes 2, 3, and 4. One constructive approach to resolving underground anger is to . . .

1. Make a list of the significant wrongs done to you over the years.
2. Analyze how you responded to each person and wound.
3. If the person isn't available or safe for you to reconcile with, then release your anger to God.
4. If you can and should talk to the person, decide whether to seek reconciliation or to let the offense go.
5. If you try to confront and reconcile, then you may need to bring a trusted third party, such as a pastor or counselor, to the meeting to act as a mediator or facilitator.
6. Aim for forgiveness. Reconciliation almost always requires forgiveness.

You can only control what you can control. You can't control whether the other person owns what he did to you or whether he asks for your forgiveness. You can control whether you let that underground anger continue to boil inside you and wreck your life from the inside out.

Reflection

- Describe a time when you felt underground anger boiling inside you or saw it in someone close to you.

- Consider the homework mini-project. How might this activity help you let go of stored anger?

- Forgiveness doesn't make the wrong okay; it makes *you* okay. In your eyes, what's the difference? What does unforgiveness or a consuming desire for revenge do to a person?

- Can you think of a classic revenge story (book, movie, or song)? What is the subliminal message about revenge? Do you buy into that message?

- When you choose to release a wrong to God, what does that show about your view of Him?

- Choosing to release a wrong to God requires courage. Why?

SCENE 5

Anger at God

On the first day of spring break, Landon slept in. (Does it even count as "sleeping in," his dad argues, if he wakes up after noon?) When he (finally) woke up, it felt like any other day. Not like his life, as he had always known it, was about to end.

He was supposed to go fishing with his grandfather, Mark, but Mark had called last evening. "Let's go later this week, Landon," his grandfather had casually said. "I scheduled a last-minute doctor's appointment." Mark had downplayed it. Classic.

When Landon's dad walked in the kitchen that afternoon, though, Landon sensed instantly that something was very wrong. Then the "let's sit down" preface. Then the delayed eye contact while his dad was fishing for the words. Then the cold, hard facts. A few words stuck in Landon's mind: the formal "your grandfather," then "stage four" and "inoperable," and finally a few miserable phrases such as "maybe a few months" and "make him comfortable." Landon went numb.

No fishing trip that week, or maybe ever. No more weekends at the ranch. No more looking up in the stands and seeing Mark's face.

Landon felt terror for his grandfather. How much pain was he in? How long had he been hiding his symptoms?

He felt sorry for his dad. After all, he would be losing his own dad.

But for himself, he just felt a gaping hole, the hole that Mark had always filled. Everyone loses people they love, but this wasn't just any other person. This was the person he had always felt closest to. The person he felt he couldn't live without. His person.

Landon's grief was pure, stage-one ANGER. And that anger had a target. Not at Mark. Not at his own dad, who was trying his best to navigate insurance and the medical system and hospice care. He felt anger—no, more like pure rage—at the One who could have protected Mark or healed him with the snap of His divine fingers.

How dare He?

Is It Okay to Feel Mad at God?

The bigger my view of God, the angrier I will get when He seems to fail me. Track this logic with me.

See, if I have a big view of God, if I believe He is who He says He is in Scripture, if I believe that He's capable of whipping out miracles that override the laws of the physical universe, if I believe that He sees and knows everything and is everywhere, then when something bad happens, I cannot help but conclude that He could have stopped it if He wanted to.

This is a common conscious and unconscious thought process that Christians experience in the face of tragedy. When Martha's brother, Lazarus, died, she looked straight at Jesus and said, "If you had been here, my brother would not have died" (John 11:21 NIV). Wow, that's bold, Martha. Often the stronger your faith, the more intense your anger toward God. Theologically, we know that God does no wrong, but emotionally we experience anger. "Why did He let this happen?" we ask.

And then some other Christians get really evasive and act as if the question itself is dangerous, too hot to handle. They stuff that question down (back to the underground anger from Act 2, Scene 4) and pretend as if God's personal brand might take a hit if we dare question Him.

I think He can handle our questions. Actually, I know He can. He can handle our desperate questions and our red-eyed rage. Our tantrums don't threaten God.

This very day, humans around the world are raising their voices to ask God a single, heartbroken question: "Why?"

Why did my little brother die from a rare form of cancer when other kids recover from the same thing?

Why did my friend die in a car accident, of all the cars on all the roads in all the world?

Why did my older sister lose her baby, when some women don't even want their children?

Why, *why*, WHY?

When Bad Things Happen Through No Fault of Your Own

Exhibit A: the story of Job. In case it's been a few years or a lifetime since you've read his story, let's do a quick synopsis.

Job was the man. The greatest, richest, most righteous, most re-spected (all these superlatives) person alive. The Bible describes him as "blameless and upright; he feared God and shunned evil" (Job 1:1 NIV). As in, this good guy deserved good things.

But sometimes bad things happen even to people like Job, de-scribed as "blameless and upright" (although I'd argue that there are zero perfectly good people; see Romans 3:10, 23). Bad things rained down on Job's innocent head. All his livestock and property stolen or incinerated. His servants murdered. All ten of his children crushed when the house where they were eating lunch together collapsed in a freak event. Job's body covered, head to toe, in painful sores. His wife encouraging him to give up. Just "curse God and die," she advised him (Job 2:9 NIV).

Crushed by grief, Job didn't sin. He didn't sling accusations at God or swear at Him or blame Him. He did, however, demand an answer to the same question, over and over and over again, spanning Job chapter 3 to chapter 37, despite his misguided friends' attempts to pin the blame on him. "God, why?!" Job roared.

This is what's so instructive for us. God did not zap Job with lightning for daring to ask the question. We can ask that question too. Job had a big view of God, so he knew that God was sovereign in his pain (see Job 1:21 and 2:10). He knew that God could have stopped the raiders, the fire, the murderers, and the mighty wind—yet He chose not to. So Job responded with what's really a heart question, not a head question: "Why, God?"

Notice that Job was allowed to ask that question, so we can too, but also notice that God refused to answer the question. That can be really hard for us to accept. God owes us no answers. God never showed Job the cards He was holding in His hand. He never told him about the cosmic showdown. Satan had bet against Job and his faith, and God had bet on him. Until the day Job died 140 years later (Job 42:16), double blessed and restored (42:10, 12), he never learned why.

He only knew the who. God's answer to Job's rage was to remind him of who He is: perfectly just, infinitely powerful, purely good, and intimately caring. "Who has a claim against me that I must pay?" God asks. "Everything under heaven belongs to me" (Job 41:11 NIV). No academic, cerebral answer would have ever satisfied Job's pain, so God gave Job the perspective to trust Him. "I know that you can do all things," Job says. "My ears had heard of you, but now my eyes have seen you" (Job 42:2a, 5 NIV). Job learned to trust God—even when, and especially when, he did not understand Him.

So are we allowed to feel angry at God? Yes.

For those of us who have a big view of a big God, is that a natural response? Double yes.

But what we do with that anger is critical.

Processing Our Anger at God

The problem with our anger at God is not the anger itself but *how we handle that anger.* "In your anger," Paul writes, "do not sin" (Ephesians 4:26 NIV). Paul doesn't dismiss the anger; he warns us to handle it with care.

Job was a master at this. "In all this," meaning *all this* pain and loss he suffered, "Job did not sin by charging God with wrongdoing" (Job 1:22 NIV; see also 2:10).

Our anger with God is distorted. I still feel real, legitimate anger over the injustice I suffered, and God gave me that capacity for anger because He stamped a sense of justice deep in my image-bearing soul. But my pain is not God's fault. True, He could have averted it. But in His wisdom and purposes He chose to allow it. Like Job, I may not understand now, but even though I experienced something wrong, that doesn't mean He is wrong.

So in my anger, I can ask Him, "Why?" He may or may not answer.

In my clouds of anger and pain, I can pour out my heart to Him (Psalm 62:8). That's what many of the psalms are—David's stream-of-consciousness, honest venting of his feelings straight to God, who listens and absorbs it all. "You have kept count of my tossings," David writes. "Put my tears in your bottle. Are they not in your book?" (Psalm 56:8 ESV). He collects my tears? Yes, He does.

Your anger doesn't surprise Him. It doesn't threaten His authority. He already knows your thoughts before you even verbalize them (Psalm 139:4), so why not just be honest with Him?

When You Feel Angry at God

So what do I tell people who feel angry at God when they come to me for counseling?

1. Take your anger directly *to* God. Openly share your feelings. As our compassionate and patient Father, God listens to our complaints. He may not give us the answers we're demanding; He may ask us to trust Him.

2. Pay attention to where He may be speaking. Sometimes God speaks in "a gentle whisper," not in the "powerful wind" or "earthquake" or "fire" we were expecting (1 Kings 19:11–12 NIV). We may hear God's voice by reading a psalm, or by talking with a friend, or by listening to a run-of-the-mill Sunday sermon, or by reading a book for English class, or by _____. (He's creative enough to fill in that blank in a thousand ways you might not expect.) His whisper will always be consistent with His Word.

3. Trust God in the darkness, just as you did in the light (see Isaiah 50:10).

4. Report for further duty. As long as you have breath in your lungs, God is not finished with you yet. Your best days are yet ahead.

Reflection

- Describe a time when you felt angry at God.

- Why do you think God doesn't always answer our questions?

- What do you take away from Job's story, which was written down as an example or warning for us (see 1 Corinthians 10:11)?

- Do you feel as if you can be completely, brutally honest with God about how you feel? Why or why not?

- What does it mean to trust God in the dark?

SCENE 6

Anger at Self

I t happens. Sometimes we just mess up—we make a bad decision, don't prepare well, try to do too much, speak unkindly or recklessly— and we can't go back. Sometimes the anger we feel isn't directed at our parents, or our siblings, or our exes, or our friends, or our circumstances, or our God. Sometimes we disappoint ourselves, and the anger we feel is directed inward. Sometimes, I'm angry at *myself*.

I Did It

Mario had locked in an offer from his dream collegiate program—a big state school, strong sense of community, beautiful campus, a young team, a chance to get playing time by his sophomore year. He had always dreamed of playing Division I football, and on signing day, he stood between his parents, who looked so proud it was almost embarrassing, and he smiled into the camera as his dream of ten-plus years fell into place. That jersey fit him perfectly.

A few months later, in a pickup game with his friends (which he had debated whether he should play in), he landed completely wrong and blew out his knee. He knew that with an emergency surgery and intense rehab he could get back on the field by the end of the fall season, but given that this was his second surgery on his right knee, he also knew the odds of doing it a third time. And he fully blamed himself.

Isabella had obsessively prepared her closing argument for the mock trial state championship. She knew every word, when to pause for effect, where to raise and lower her volume, how to make the right amount of eye contact with the judges, and how to win the crowd. She had never felt so ready. But something felt *off* that day, and Isabella never got in her groove. Her nerves made her voice sound shaky. Once she thought about her shaky voice, she could only think about her delivery, and then she lost her content. Entire lines and points erased from her mind, poof! The other team had Supreme Court judge look-alike as their coach, and the students dressed in designer suits. (Who *are* these people?) Her team looked pathetically wrinkly and frumpy, and once Isabella let that cold insecurity snake around her heart, her confidence was shot. When her team lost, her teammates barely looked at her, which confirmed what she knew all along: it was her fault.

For his junior year, which is notoriously and universally stressful, Jacob overcommitted himself. All seven AP and dual-credit classes. A part-time job (which his counselor had advised him would look impressive on his college applications). One student club. Two varsity sports. No life, really, just a heavy weight of pressure around his neck, pulling him under. As Jacob clawed to retain his top ten rank, which he knew was a nonnegotiable for the two colleges he had his eye on, he let stress cloud his judgment. On a Thursday night at 1:00 a.m., he stared bleary-eyed at his laptop screen, willing his one anemic paragraph to grow into a five-page literary analysis essay. So he took the AI shortcut, and he justified it to himself. Two weeks later, when Ms. Stone posted the grades, his stomach dropped when he saw that zero. He knew just how much that single grade would cost him, and he had no one to blame but himself.

For two years Lucas and Aria had been labeled "the perfect couple." Most relationships don't even last two years, but theirs was textbook. They spent time together, but they didn't smother each other. They went to each other's games and performances, texted constantly, and got along with each other's families. In the yearbook survey, they were voted Most Likely to Get Married, and maybe they would. They never rushed things and just seemed so chill together. But then Lucas made a mistake. A mistake named Emma, and the gossip seeped out like a poison fog until it finally reached Aria, who was heartbroken but who had enough dignity to end the relationship, full stop. Her choice was final and irrevocable, not a "well, let's just see," but more of a "you're not the person I thought you were, and this chapter of our lives is over." Every time Lucas sees Aria, he knows what he lost. Not that she was perfect, but she was perfect for him. And losing her was 100 percent his fault.

Tristan was rushing to practice. He was running a little late, and Coach had threatened to make the whole team run if they weren't all on the field on time. Tristan sped through a yellow light, felt his phone vibrate, glanced down for a split second to check his team's WhatsApp messages, and managed to bump the back of a slow-moving minivan in front of him. He felt furious with himself. "I can't believe I just did that," he fumed. He feared his dad's reaction and his coach's reaction, but his worst critic was himself. He didn't have the money to repair his dad's Bronco, let alone some soccer mom's aging Honda Odyssey. "I'm an idiot," he thought.

That was an accident, a careless mistake. What infuriates us even more is when we violate our own values—like Jacob's academic dishonesty or Lucas's cheating on his girlfriend. Maya has a story like that too. Maya has always had a healthy, open relationship with her parents. So many of her friends hate their parents (or so they claim) or simply ignore them. Some parents do that free-range, raise-yourself thing. Others hover and smother. Hers are just normal. They eat family dinners together, they ask her questions about her life because they're interested, and they trust her. The fact that she started lying to them about where she's been going on Friday nights (*not* to her friend Tessa's house, for the record) makes her feel like dirt. "Why did I do that? I didn't even have to lie to them."

What is Maya feeling? Guilt. Vintage, vanilla-bean, straight-up guilt. Which is actually a healthy sign, because guilt is designed to lead us to fix things, to ask for forgiveness, and to make things right. When we harden our hearts so much that we don't feel guilt, then that's a sign that our hearts are calcifying. At the same time, when we lacerate ourselves so much that we wallow in our guilt, that's also an unhealthy response.

I'm the Problem

Most of us know that pain of being angry with ourselves. Like Taylor Swift, we admit, "It's me, hi, I'm the problem, it's me." When those flashes of self-anger come, it's usually because we perceive that we did something wrong. We acted carelessly, foolishly, or irresponsibly. In the heat of this self-anger, we may feel some mix of guilt, shame, condemnation, and even self-hatred if we let that one choice cloud our entire sense of identity.

Remember, anger is an emotional and physical response of intense displeasure when we encounter someone or something that we perceive to be wrong, unfair, or unjust. Even if that someone is me! Sometimes *I* am the one guilty of the wrong choice, the unkindness, the injustice, or the carelessness. Sometimes *I* fall far short of my own expectations.

How *Not* to Process Self-Anger

Let's take a quick quiz. Label each of these responses **H** for healthy or **U** for unhealthy.

_____ The extreme: "My life is useless! I wish I were dead."

_____ The blame game: "I wouldn't have felt like I had to do that if you weren't so controlling."

_____ The hiding: "I feel so ashamed of myself. I can never face the world again."

Did you label each of those **U** (for unhealthy)? I hope so! I'm sure you can add more terrible responses to that list. Explosions at those around us (from Act 2, Scene 3). The urge to self-harm. A loop of silent mental attacks: "I deserve to suffer, look what I did, I was so stupid, I don't know why anybody would believe in me again, I knew that was wrong, I still did it anyway, I don't deserve forgiveness, I don't deserve to be happy ever again, repeat repeat repeat."

All in favor of a healthier option?

How to Process Self-Anger

Are you angry at yourself? If not now, someday you will be. Someday you'll fail someone you love, or let your bank account get hacked, or wreck your car—or worse, run over someone's puppy with your car—or make a bad choice, or say something you desperately wish you could take back. Such is life. We all fail. When that happens . . .

1. Admit your anger. Write it down if necessary. Verbalize it to God in prayer.

2. Objectively examine your anger. Is it justified—or are you loading yourself with needless guilt and shame? (For example, a victim of abuse might feel she should have done something to prevent it, but that is not on her at all.)

3. If your anger toward yourself is valid, then confess your wrong choices to God, and accept His forgiveness.

4. Choose to forgive yourself rather than berate yourself. If you have asked for and accepted God's forgiveness, then through prayer, ask God to help you let it go. Memorize Psalm 32:1 and all of Psalm 51.

5. Learn from your failures. We all make mistakes. What defines us is what we do after we make those mistakes. Set safeguards in your life so you won't repeat those mistakes again.

Reflection

- Describe a time when you felt angry at yourself. As you look back now, how do you perceive your level of self-anger then, in the moment?

- When you feel angry at yourself, does it tend to be over an accident (e.g., you wrecked your car), a failure (e.g., you missed the game-winning free throw or bombed your PSAT), or a moral mistake (e.g., you lied to your parents)? What patterns do you notice?

- When we feel self-anger, many of us react with an extreme. How well are you able to keep things in perspective when you feel the weight of guilt or regret? We must learn from our mistakes, but we can't let them define us.

- What steps do you need to take to process your self-anger in a healthy way so that you can move on with your life?

Act 3

MAKING THINGS RIGHT

Forgiveness ≠ Restitution

There are no enduring human relationships without forgiveness. Think about any long-lasting relationship. Six months of dating. A friendship that lasts all through middle school and high school. Business partners for decades. Siblings for life. Marriage till death do us part. In every long-term relationship, one person *will* fail the other. One person will hurt the other's feelings. One person will disappoint the other. One person will break the other's heart. One person will run her mouth when she should have kept silent. As humans, our failure is inevitable. Some people discard any relationship as soon as it gets complicated. They live in a perpetual rotation of new, shallow relationships. They always have the high of a new crush, never the depth of knowing someone and of being known for the long haul. That's a sad and shallow way to live.

In order to preserve any relationship for the long haul, we have to learn the art of the apology. Fortunately for us, this skill can be learned.

"Sprechen Sie Englisch?"

When it comes to apologizing, people speak different languages. This is not a literal language clash, where person A rattles off a phrase in German while person B is listening closely for English words. This is a communication clash, where person A's words do not register for person B at all. What person A considers a sincere apology falls flat for person B, who hears forced, insincere words. Person A thinks he apologized, but person B is still waiting to hear that golden apology. Person A wants to move on, while person B is still stuck in the conflict.

In our counseling practices, Dr. Jennifer Thomas and I have noticed this pattern with our clients. Every client falls in one of five categories, and we labeled these the five languages of apology. You have a native apology language—how you naturally express your apologies, and what you naturally listen for when someone apologizes to you. Here's a quick preview; we will explore each of these in more depth in the upcoming Scenes:

Language of Apology	Sounds like
#1: Regret	"I'm sorry."
#2: Responsibility	"I was wrong."
#3: Restitution	"How can I make it up to you?"
#4: Repentance/Change	"I will try not to do that ever again."
#5: Request	"Will you forgive me?"

Wait a Second. Can You Forgive Without an Apology?

Yes. And no.

Before we get into the five apology languages, this is a sticky point we should consider. The first formula I want you to learn is this:

FORGIVENESS ≠ RESTITUTION

Remember that ≠ symbol from math class? Forgiveness does not equal restitution. These are two separate things, and we have to deal with them separately.

Forgiveness is releasing the person from the harm he caused you. You choose not to take revenge or demand justice; you leave all that in God's hands and move on. That may be a onetime choice, or it may be a cyclical process that you return to many times. Sometimes you have to choose to forgive, and forgive, and forgive seventy-seven times to really let go of that one offense (see Matthew 18:21–22). For really deep wounds, such as abuse or neglect or abandonment, I highly recommend you work with a therapist or pastor to help coach you through the process so you don't have to navigate it alone. This takes courage, but it's definitely worth it. We are commanded to forgive, not only because it's the right thing to do (see Matthew 6:12–15), but also because unforgiveness will tear us up inside. Forgive so that you can be free.

Restitution is fixing the relationship. And that is not required by God and may not be wise. Now I'm not telling you to casually discard relationships, because you should fight to preserve your core relationships in life. But I am telling you that if someone intentionally hurt you, and that person has shown no remorse, then that person may be emotionally or even physically dangerous for you, and you should keep your distance. Again, a wise outside perspective can help you see the broken relationship more clearly. Find a pastor, counselor, or savvy adult who will tell you what you need to hear, not just what you want to hear. If the relationship can and should be repaired, then do your part to fix it. If the relationship is broken and unsafe, then let that one float out to sea.

Cheap Forgiveness

Forgiveness comes at a high price and should be respected for what it is: a minor miracle here on earth.

Some Christians try to cheapen the idea of forgiveness. A well-meaning Christian might dismissively tell a victim of abuse, "Just forgive and move on already." Umm, that's a hard no. That's not the way forgiveness works.

We are to follow Jesus' pattern, "forgiving each other, just as in Christ God forgave you" (Ephesians 4:32 NIV). But how exactly does God forgive us? If we confess our sins, He freely forgives (see 1 John 1:9). But nowhere in the Old or New Testaments do we see God handing out forgiveness tokens to people who don't care enough to ask for them.

Let's apply that to human relationships. What if the person who hurt you never apologizes? Sadly that happens all too often. The wounded person can't hold on to that sense of injury for her whole life; it will eat her alive. For her own sake, she must forgive, then release the person to God for justice, then release her anger to God for healing. But she does not have to restore her relationship with the person who hurt her. You can't rush that process, and you can't force restitution.

Genuine apologies and forgiveness remove the barrier that was created by the offense and clear the path to restoring trust over time. If the relationship was close before the offense, it can grow close again. If the relationship was simply a casual acquaintance, then it may or may not ever grow deeper. If the offense was perpetrated by an unknown person, such as a rapist, then there is no relationship to be restored. Remember, too, that forgiveness does not erase consequences. Even if the rapist sincerely apologizes, he should still face harsh judicial consequences. Let's not cheapen forgiveness.

The Five-Gallon Container

Picture your conscience as a five-gallon container strapped to your back. Whenever you wrong someone else, it's like pouring a gallon of water into your conscience. Three or four wrongs, and your conscience is getting full—and that container is feeling heavy. That's a tough way to live, hauling that weight of guilt and unresolved conflict around with you everywhere. The only way to effectively empty your conscience is to apologize to God and to the person you hurt. Only then can you look God in the face, look yourself in the mirror, and look the other person in the eyes—not because you're perfect, but because you're willing to take responsibility for your failures.

Are you good at apologizing? Not yet? Well, read on then. Some people learned the art of the apology when they were kids. In healthy families, parents teach their children to apologize, and those parents apologize to their own children when they fail. It's a healthy cycle. Many children, however, grow up in dysfunctional families where pain, anger, and unforgiveness are the norm. Can they learn to apologize? Yes, but as with any new skill in life, they have to work at it.

Remember . . .

Humanity has an amazing capacity to forgive. Don't underestimate yourself.

Love often means saying you're sorry.

Forgiveness ≠ restitution.

There are no enduring human relationships without forgiveness.

And forgiveness sets you free. All in favor of freedom? Let's go learn the art of the apology.

Reflection

- Scan back over the list of reminders you just read. What stands out to you, and why?

- Consider your family of origin. How well did your parents/grandparents/key adults model the art of apologizing? When they were wrong, did they admit it? What did you learn from their example (or non-example)?

- What is the link between forgiveness and freedom?

- Why did we spend a chunk of time differentiating between forgiveness and restitution? Why is it important for us to perceive those as two distinct things?

- When you hear an apology, how do you know whether it's genuine or fake?

- As you read this chapter, what relationships came to mind that need the elixir of apology and forgiveness?

SCENE 1

The Language of Regret

Have you ever heard a movie reference that you just didn't get—because you never saw that movie?

Have you ever been to a concert where every other fan is singing along with the lyrics—but you don't even know that song?

Have you ever gotten to a section on a test and realized with horror—uh oh, I skipped that section of the study guide entirely?

Sometimes we're missing context or knowledge, or we just don't get it. Not for lack of effort, but somewhere along the way there was a disconnect.

Sometimes our apologies land like that too. As in, they miss the target entirely. We might think we're sincerely apologizing, but on the receiving end, the person hears . . . silence. Why is that?

Genuine or Fake?

What most people are listening for in an apology is *sincerity*. They want to hear a genuine apology, but how do they judge sincerity? How do they read the other person's heart and motives? This is tricky.

As I've said, this ambiguity led Jennifer Thomas and me to study the five basic elements of an apology and then to conclude that there are five apology languages. You have a native language. So do I. So does your sister. So do your stepdad, your best friend, your volleyball coach. And if we want to be effective in our relationships, we have to learn to speak each other's languages. For most people, one or two of these languages sound way more sincere than the others. In order to effectively apologize, you might not use all five apology languages in a single apology, but you do need to speak the language that communicates your sincerity to the person you hurt. In other words, think how the words you're speaking will come across to the recipient. Then, and only then, will that person hear your apology as genuine and accept your words.

All five languages are equal. There's not one dazzling language and one droll language. There's no right or wrong or hierarchy. Some of these will resonate more with you than others, but in order to keep your relationships healthy, you will have to learn to speak all five so you can communicate with your people.

LANGUAGE 1

The first language of apology is expressing regret, and the language sounds like this: "I am sorry." Basic? Yes. Powerful? Remarkably so.

Expressing regret conveys the *emotional* aspect of an apology. When you say those magic words, "I'm sorry," you express that you get it—you understand how you hurt your friend and what that felt like. Expressing regret is fundamental to good relationships.

Because we care about the other person, we regret the pain we caused him or her. We don't want that person to feel the hurt, the disappointment, the inconvenience, the betrayal. Regret focuses on what you did (or failed to do) and how that emotionally affected the other person. You feel their pain. They're listening for evidence that you realize how deeply you hurt them. For some people, this is the only thing they listen for in an apology. Without hearing those words of regret, they label the apology insincere. A simple "I'm sorry" can go a long way toward making things right.

Case Study

Graduation can have some complicated and weird dynamics. Miles, Justin, and Sebastian had been friends for years, like the three musketeers, some called them. Then the moms got involved. Justin's mom and Sebastian's mom started planning a graduation party for them. Their families were friends, and the moms were actually in business together. They ran a catering business, so it was natural to them to put on an event for their two boys. They sent out a joint invitation. No harm meant—but no Miles mentioned. Sure, they *invited* him to Justin and Sebastian's party along with other friends, but they didn't see any reason to make it a party for three; it was two families planning a celebration for their sons.

Well, the whole thing made Justin and Sebastian feel awkward, but they didn't say anything because they didn't want to make it worse. When it finally got so weird that they had to address it with Miles, they explained to him all the reasons why it just happened that way. Miles listened with an open mind. He didn't want to blow up their friendship over something petty. He scanned through the whole conversation listening for two words, those two simple words that would have told him that they got it, those two words that Miles never heard.

"I'm sorry" would have made a world of difference to Miles.

"I'm sorry" would have communicated that his two friends cared that he felt left out.

"I'm sorry" would have conveyed that, while the moms ran away with it, the sons could have intervened.

"I'm sorry" would have spoken the emotional language of an emotional human being at a major transition point in his life.

~~Disconnect~~

Let's consider some factors that negate your apologies, and let's actively avoid them, like the plague. We'll take a hard pass on ~~Disconnect~~, ~~Vagueness~~, ~~But~~, and ~~Manipulation~~ (which is why we crossed each of these words out). Let's start with verbal-nonverbal disconnect.

Do your nonverbal cues agree with your words?

If I want my "I'm sorry" to sound genuine, then my body language must match. If my body is screaming aggression, tension, and conflict (my arms are crossed, my expression looks closed, and I'm leaning forward), then my two messages clash. In contrast, if my tone sounds soft and if I convey openness and humility in my posture, then my body language matches my words—and my message goes through.

Like these two savvy sisters who are masters of reading nonverbal cues. Lily can easily read Lucy. When I asked her, "How do you know if Lucy's apology is sincere?" Lily replied, "Eye contact. If she looks me in the eye when she says she's sorry, I know she actually means it. If she blows through the room and says, 'I'm sorry,' without even pausing to look at me, then I know she's hiding something."

And not *like the coach* who screams, "I said I was sorry!" I'm going out on a limb to guess he's . . . not.

~~Vagueness~~

Let's also avoid vagueness.

An apology has more impact when it's *specific*. For what, exactly, are you sorry?

Let's say your friend Reagan was supposed to meet you to go see a movie, and she showed up forty-five minutes late. For no good reason. Which response rings true?

"Sorry," Reagan whispers as she sits down next to you in the theater, and that's the end of it. Even after the closing credits, when you look at her with an inquisitively raised eyebrow, she just says "sorry" again and abruptly changes the topic to sushi.

Or . . .

"Sorry," Reagan whispers as she sits down next to you in the theater, and she adds, "I'll explain more later." Reagan knows how much you love movies and doesn't want to interrupt your experience. After the movie ends, she goes on. "I am sorry. I know that must have been so annoying when I wasn't even returning your messages. Knowing you, you probably got here early and were worried about me and might have even missed the previews because you were still waiting for me. No excuses—my bad. I'm sorry if I ruined your night."

It's not the word count of the second apology. It's that the specific details reveal that she gets it and understands the emotional annoyance and inconvenience she caused. It sounds sincere, and you're much more likely to accept that apology and move on, and maybe even get sushi.

~~"But . . ."~~

Sincere regret also needs to stand alone. It should not be followed by the dreaded "but."

Not this: "I'm sorry I lost my temper with you, but you started it."

Simply this: "I'm sorry I lost my temper with you."

Not this: "I'm sorry I ditched you at the party, but you should have been more aware of how I was feeling."

Simply this: "I'm sorry I ditched you at the party."

Not this: "I'm sorry I hurt your feelings, but I've had a horrible day."

Simply this: "I'm sorry I hurt your feelings."

Avoid the "but"! Adding the "but" is one of those terrible human instincts. Anytime we verbally shift the blame to the other person, we have moved from an apology to an attack. Attacks never lead to forgiveness and reconciliation. Own your part, and let the other person choose to own his or her own part, or not. You can't control the other person's apology, but you can control yours. Let the apology stand alone.

~~Manipulation~~

An expression of sincere regret should not manipulate the other person into reciprocating.

Molly and Owen have been dating for almost a year. In some ways they're compatible, but in other ways, they just can't connect. Molly says, "Sometimes Owen will say he's sorry, but then he just looks at me and waits. He expects me to say it back, even if I don't feel like I should have to because this fight was all on him. This just isn't working for me. I want him to say he's sorry. Period. Not expecting anything in return. Then I would know he's truly sorry." The expectation trap ruins the apology.

So does a wrong motivation. If someone apologizes only to get you off his back, then that's not a sincere apology. We have to make sure our motives are true. That we're sorry. That we understand the pain we caused. Not that we want to manipulate the other person.

The Little Blue Dots

Can you text your apology? You have to read the dynamic on this one. Sometimes the only way to repair a relationship is face-to-face. Sometimes you have to look your friend/brother/aunt/girlfriend/coach in the eye and say, "I'm sorry." Sometimes the nature of the relationship and the style of the conflict allow for a written apology, which might allow you to put a lot of thought into your words and give them real emotional weight. As always, be sincere and be specific, and as always, be careful what you put in writing in case it takes on a life of its own.

Recap

To review, for some individuals in your life, and you have to figure out who they are, a sincere "I'm sorry" is the clearest language of apology. Your "I'm sorry" speaks to their emotions and acknowledges the link between your rotten behavior and their pain. Your regret assures them that you're sincere, and your identification with their pain primes them to forgive and drive on. Without those magic words, they're stuck in neutral.

Language 1 is Regret, and it can sound like this:

"I know now that I hurt you very deeply. It hurts me to think about how I hurt you. I am truly sorry."

"I feel really bad that I disappointed you. I should have been more thoughtful. I'm sorry that I caused you pain."

"At the time, I was obviously not thinking clearly. I never intended to hurt you, but now I can see I was way out of line. I'm sorry I was so insensitive."

"I'm sorry I violated your trust. I understand that even after I apologize, it may take a while for you to trust me again."

Reflection

- Is Language 1: Regret your primary language of apology? Meaning, when someone apologizes to you, do you find yourself listening for the words "I'm sorry"? How central do those two words seem to you?

- "Expressing regret conveys the *emotional* aspect of an apology." Why is this first language, Regret, tied to emotions?

- Review the section titles of what *not* to do (which is why we crossed them out—get it?): ~~Disconnect~~, ~~Vagueness~~, ~~But~~, and ~~Manipulation~~. Which of those are you sometimes tempted to do? And which one sets you off when you're on the receiving end?

- What idea(s) will you take away from this chapter to help you better heal your relationships?

SCENE 2

The Language of Responsibility

He didn't feel well. She had barely slept. His friends always expected too much. Her teacher hadn't explained the assignment. His siblings were impossible. She just couldn't help what she had done . . .

A Consistent Theme

Coach Wells usually had enough patience to deal with sixteen-year-old boys, but on this particular Tuesday, with playoffs approaching, he snapped. "If you ever do that again," he screamed at Ryan, who had misjudged the arc of the ball from the punt and had made a rare mistake, "I will cut you from this team."

Everyone heard it: the players on the field, the subs, the trainers, the residents of the next county east. Ryan would never forget those words. Coach Wells felt guilty the moment the words left his mouth. He felt frustrated with the whole team, not just with Ryan, but his explosion was directed solely at Ryan. True, he wanted leaders like Ryan to focus more. "This will make him mentally stronger," Coach told himself. "He needs to be able to handle criticism. He can't be soft." But inside, Coach knew he'd overreacted. He just couldn't bring himself to say, "I was wrong."

Jada struggled with time. Her mom always teased her that her worst flaw was her punctuality (or lack of punctuality). School starts at 8:30 in the morning? Jada floats in at 8:37. A 3:30 p.m. rehearsal?

Look for Jada by four. But the one place where she knew she had to be on time was work. Since she started working at First Watch, Jada had been setting a double alarm on her phone to make sure she got to the restaurant in time to park and clock in before her shift started. She usually came tearing in at the last minute. But it seemed inevitable that she would eventually be late to a shift, if not outright oversleep and miss it. When she burst into the restaurant forty-five minutes late on a Saturday morning, during a particularly busy rush, her manager, Callie, looked at her with a mix of disappointment and irritation. They were already short-staffed, so why had Jada put them in this position? Jada felt mad at herself, but her mind immediately shifted to all the reasons it wasn't her fault. Confusing messages on Slack. Her mom's rule that Jada's iPhone had to be in her parents' room at night. Her older brother's extra long shower. Meanwhile Callie and the other servers felt as if Jada owed them an apology for showing up late again, but Jada just couldn't bring herself to say, "My fault. I'm sorry."

Unfortunately for Antonio, his collarbone fracture was not a clean break. In a cloud of pain medication, he kept shifting in his recliner, trying to get into a comfortable position. Every four hours, his mom hovered over him, refilling his water, delivering his next round of meds, offering him more toast. "Just checking on you," she'd say, buzzing around him like a frantic bee. Unfortunately for her, Antonio's pain overcame his patience, and he snapped at her to get away and to, umm, relocate her toast. Immediately he felt that stab of guilt. "Unkind," he thought. "Ungrateful," he admitted to himself. "But medicine can make anyone act crazy. My mom needs to give me space." He averted his eyes from his mom's wounded expression so he wouldn't have to apologize.

Three different scenarios: screaming mean words, failing to come through for others, lashing out at someone innocent.

One consistent theme: an unwillingness to say the words "I was wrong."

Coach Wells, Jada, and Antonio all covered their need to apologize with excuses, stifling their feelings of guilt. A simple apology could have reset each of those scenarios, but that would have meant accepting responsibility for their actions, and for some people, that is really hard to do.

Why is it so difficult for some of us to say, "I was wrong"? This is not a rhetorical question. Honestly, why can some people not spit those words out? There's actually a reason. Our reluctance to admit wrongdoing may be tied to our sense of self-worth. To admit we're wrong may be perceived as a weakness. We may reason, "Only losers air their mistakes. Intelligent people can justify their way out of anything."

Some people are conditioned this way from childhood. If a child is overly punished or shamed every time he makes a tiny mistake, he quickly learns to hide his mistakes. One mistake diminishes his sense of self-worth, so he subconsciously links wrong behavior with low self-worth. If he gets caught making a mistake, then he's a "bad" person. The kid who grows up with this emotional pattern will have difficulty admitting wrongdoing when he's older because to admit imperfection strikes at his own self-esteem.

Can this negative pattern be broken? Absolutely! Mature teens learn to accept responsibility for their own choices, and their self-esteem is resilient enough to absorb their imperfections. Immature teens are forever rationalizing their choices so they don't have to face their own imperfections (or consequences).

"Not My Fault"

Have you ever felt the urge to rationalize your choices? Blame someone else? Justify your mistakes? These are all signs of immaturity.

In contrast: Swallowing your pride and admitting, "I was wrong." Accepting responsibility for your own choices. Having a strong enough sense of self to flex with your good and bad days. These are all signs of maturity.

Agree/Disagree

Try this technique to help you sort out your feelings vs. your choices. It might sound cheesy at first, but it's actually helped many people.

I *agree* that I have a right to feel hurt, angry, disappointed, frustrated, or whatever else I may be feeling. I don't choose my feelings; I simply experience them.

I *disagree* with the idea that because of my feelings, I have the right to hurt someone else with my words or choices. To hurt my best friend because my best friend hurt me is like declaring civil war, a war in which there are no winners.

You can't control your feelings; but you can control your choices. So no matter what you are feeling, choose to respond in a way that doesn't set off a nuclear explosion in your life, wiping out all signs of life in a ten-mile radius.

Yes?

Yes!

LANGUAGE 2

Which leads us to the powerful second apology language: Responsibility. It sounds like this: "I was wrong. That's on me. My fault." For native speakers of the Responsibility language, when they hear an apology, they are listening for some version of those ownership words. We have to accept responsibility for our choices, and we have to have the courage to verbalize that.

Reuben and his dad are at an impasse over this very issue. "My dad will never admit he made a mistake," Reuben said. "If I bring it up, he snaps at me and asks why I can't move on. If he could just admit he was wrong, just once, I'd be willing to forgive him." Instead, the resentment between the two of them just keeps building. "My dad's a hypocrite," Reuben explained. "He's revered as this successful business leader, but he has never once apologized to my mom or me. That's why I try to be the first to admit when I was wrong. I don't want to be like him."

Daisy had an opposite experience at home. Growing up, she often heard her parents apologize to each other and to her. "We all make mistakes," they told her. "What matters is what you do after you make a mistake." For the past twenty years, Daisy has seen her imperfect parents own their mistakes. "I was wrong. I'm sorry I snapped at you. My fault for forgetting to fill the car with gas. I was late to pick you up today, Daisy, and that's my bad." The air between them is clear not because her parents are any better humans than Reuben's dad, but because they feel comfortable admitting they were wrong. "Admitting mistakes is part of our family culture," Daisy said with a shrug. "I owe that to my parents."

Recap

To Reuben and to Daisy and to many others, hearing the apology language of accepting responsibility for one's wrong choices is the most important part of an apology. Without that note of responsibility, the apology falls flat.

Language 2 is Responsibility, and it can sound like this:

"I know what I did was wrong. No excuses. Honestly, what I did was selfish and wrong."

"My fault."

"I made a big mistake. I wasn't really thinking through what I was doing, but in retrospect, I wish I had thought before I acted. What I did was wrong."

"The way I spoke to you was wrong. It was harsh and untrue. I was trying to justify myself, and the way I talked to you was unkind and unloving. I hope you will forgive me."

"I repeated a mistake we've discussed before. I know that it was 100 percent my fault."

Reflection

- Is Language 2: Responsibility your primary language of apology? Meaning, when someone apologizes to you, do you find yourself listening for the words "That was my fault"? How central does that ownership seem to you?

- How comfortable are you with taking responsibility for your actions? Do you find yourself tempted to make excuses, rationalize your choices, or blame others?

- Why is the ability to admit your mistakes and own them a sign of maturity?

- As you read this chapter, who comes to your mind as good at admitting personal faults? Who comes to mind as unwilling to own personal mistakes?

- What idea(s) will you take away from this chapter to help you better heal your relationships?

The Language of Restitution

The most famous story of restitution happened two thousand-ish years ago. Has your mind raced there yet?

More hints: a vertically challenged (translation: extra-short), drippingly wealthy (translation: actively thieving), absolutely hated man (translation: a friendless, chief tax collector). With me yet?

Zacchaeus. You can read his full story in Luke 19, but here's the quick version: This detested man met Jesus, and his whole life changed. Jesus has that effect, you know? Because of his heart change, Zacchaeus decided to make things right in his life. "Look, Lord!" he said to Jesus. "Here and now I give half of my possessions to the poor, and if I have cheated anybody out of anything, I will pay back four times the amount" (Luke 19:8 NIV). Now *that* is restitution.

If you look at the word *restitution*, it might remind you of the word *restore*, and that's exactly what it means: restoring something to its rightful owner and making things even again. Our human psyches naturally long for this. If a friend borrows my car, I expect him to refill it with gas. If I treat my friend for boba this time, she might pick up the tab the next time. Those cases seem clear-cut.

This concept of restitution is embedded in the American justice system, and it just makes sense. The punishment should match the crime. Theft? Pay the money back. Graffiti? Clean the wall. At-fault car accident? Pay the other driver's repair costs.

But then it gets a little murkier. What about the person who steals a boyfriend or girlfriend? How can that be made right? Or the person who slanders me and sullies my reputation? Or even more extreme cases: murder or rape? Some crimes can't be undone, and no earthly price would ever rebalance those scales.

"Still Love Me?"

In the public arena, our emphasis on restitution is based on a shared sense of justice. The one who commits the crime should pay to fix it. In the private sphere of personal relationships, our desire for restitution is almost always tied to our need for love. After being hurt deeply, we need the reassurance that the person who hurt us still loves us.

After all, why is it that the people who can hurt us the most are the people we love the most? If a stranger or a mere acquaintance says something critical to me, I can brush that off, but if it's a sibling or a parent or close friend, I feel, "You cut me deep, bro. You cut me real deep just now." My brother's harsh criticism calls into question his love for me. "How could he love me yet say those cruel words?" I wonder. And a quick "sorry" does not answer the heart question, "Do you still love me?" This question demands a dose of restitution.

LANGUAGE 3

And for some people, Restitution is their primary apology language. If they hear, "I'm sorry" (Regret) and even "I was wrong" (Responsibility), they are still listening for more: "What can I do to make things right?" or "How can I show you that I still value you?" That's the crux of *Restitution*.

This reality surfaced again and again in our research. The heart desire for restitution sounds something like this:

"I expect him to try to repair what went wrong."

"I expect her to be truly sorry from the heart and be willing to make things right."

"I want him to make amends. Things don't just go away by saying the words 'I'm sorry.'"

For people who speak this third apology language, actions speak louder than words. They view the effort to make restitution as evidence of the sincerity of the apology.

Okay, but How?

So how exactly do we go about making restitution? The goal is to restore the relationship, rebalance the scales of justice, and reassure someone close that I still care about him or her. In order to hit the bull's-eye, I need to speak that person's love language. Restitution is not one-size-fits-all. We have to tailor the restitution to the person we hurt. Think about the cliché husband who, no matter what he's done this time, shows up with a cheap bouquet of flowers to apologize to his wife. She might not even like flowers, and what might speak to her more is a thoughtful note (Words) or simply vacuuming the crushed Goldfish and Cheerios off her car floor (Service). We have to think about the person we're trying to patch things up with and figure out what speaks to him or her. Make sense? For more on this, read *A Teen's Guide to the 5 Love Languages*. For now, let's distill some ideas into a simple form.

Love Language	Definition	Ideas for restitution
Words	Using words to affirm the other person.	Using positive words to make up for damaging words. Examples: • "Here are some of my favorite things about you." • "I'll always be here for you."
Service	Demonstrating love by thoughtful acts of kindness.	Finding a creative way to serve the person you hurt. Examples: • Helping your little brother with his math homework. • Driving your friend to his physical therapy appointment.
Gifts	Showing that you thought about the person by giving him or her a gift. Price is irrelevant—maximize the thoughtfulness.	Surprising the person you offended with a thoughtful gift. Examples: • Your best friend's favorite Starbucks drink. • A magnet for your sister's collection.
Time	Giving another person your *undivided* attention, which communicates, "You're that important to me."	Planning a special event for the person you hurt. Examples: • Going for a walk with your mom in the evening and actually asking about her day. • Shopping with your best friend for her homecoming dress.
Touch	Communicating personal connection and reassurance through casual physical touch.	Following up a verbal apology with a physical expression. Examples: • Throwing your arm across your little brother's shoulders. • Hugging your mom after you apologize to her.

Let's illustrate. Let's say you just watched WWIII play out between your dad and your brother, who is, let's face it, being a punk. But your dad, at his wits' end, crossed the line and actually hurt Grayson's feelings. Your dad accused your brother of being lazy and irresponsible and then made the mistake of comparing him to you. ("Don't drag *me* into this!" you were thinking.) By that point, Grayson, who usually seems tough, fell apart. Your dad apologized, but it wasn't until he walked over to him and gave him a big bear hug that Grayson's face relaxed with relief. Then, and only then, did the apology register with Grayson, and that's because your dad was savvy enough to speak your brother's love language: Touch. The hug was his restitution—simple, free, and effective—and Grayson felt reaffirmed.

Recap

Sometimes "I'm sorry" (Regret) and even "all my fault" (Responsibility) are not enough. Sometimes you have to make amends (Restitution) in order to make things right.

If you borrow your sister's hoodie and then lose it, you can't just tell her you're sorry. Buy her a new hoodie! That's a fair expectation in life.

If you neglect your best friends because you are spending too much time with your new girlfriend, their teasing won't stop if you just say, "My bad." Spend time with them! Another fair expectation in life.

If you hurt your mom's feelings by comparing her to Greg's amazing mom, then "sorry" isn't enough. Tell her something specific she does that you really appreciate (like cooking a healthy dinner for you).

When you can, make things right. Language 3 is Restitution, and it can sound like this:

"Is there anything I can do to make up for what I have done?"

"I know I hurt you deeply, and I feel like I should do something to repay you. Any suggestions?"

"It doesn't feel like enough to just say, 'I'm sorry.' I want to make up for what I've done. Any ideas for how I can rebalance the scales?"

"I know I've inconvenienced you. May I give you some of my time to balance things out?"

"I regret that I damaged your reputation. I'm going to post something good about you."

Reflection

- Is Language 3: Restitution your primary language of apology? Meaning, when someone apologizes to you, do you find yourself listening for the words "How can I make things right?" How essential does that rebalancing seem to you?

- Review the chart of the 5 love languages. Which is your primary language? What acts of restitution speak most clearly to you?

- Think about your five closest relationships. Which is the primary love language for each of them? Now apply that to restitution: when you apologize, how can you tailor your restitution so it fits the person?

- What idea(s) will you take away from this chapter to help you better heal your relationships?

SCENE 4

The Language of Repentance

Sofia and Malik have the same old argument on a repeating loop. "Conflict is normal," Sofia tells herself. "Everyone fights sometimes." True, but what bothers her isn't the presence of conflict—she likes how honest they are with each other and how well they can talk things out—it's that they never seem to make progress. Nothing changes.

Here's the pattern: They'll make plans to spend a Saturday together. Malik will pick Sofia up. "Where to?" he'll ask.

"I don't care. You pick," Sofia will answer. And they sit there, car running, poised for a fun day out, directionless as always. Eventually, forty *s-l-o-w* minutes later, Sofia will rescue their afternoon: "I heard about a new restaurant in the city," she'll say, or "Let's go climbing." Laid-back Malik will agree, of course. He always agrees.

He just never asserts.

Or plans.

Or takes initiative in any way, shape, or form.

Never one to bury conflict, Sofia will address the issue. "Malik? Would you be willing to plan our next date? It just feels as if you don't . . . care how I feel."

And then he'll minimize her concern, brush it aside, and reassure her that next time, oh next time, things will be different.

But they never are. Same scene, on repeat.

"Nobody's perfect," Sofia reminds herself, thinking of all the qualities she likes about Malik. Seriously, in the grand scheme of things, isn't Malik's passivity just a little thing? But if he really cared about her, wouldn't he take her feelings seriously and make a change?

LANGUAGE 4

Fair expectation? I think so. Sofia wants Malik to *repent*. That's an old-fashioned word, but there's no modern word that quite captures the idea. To repent is to do a one-eighty. To change your mind. To stop walking due south and pivot to true north. In the context of apologies, it means that an individual realizes that his present patterns are destructive, regrets the pain he is causing the other person, and chooses to drastically change his behavior.

Think about the progression of apologies we've been learning: "I'm sorry" = Regret. "I was wrong" = Responsibility. "How can I make it up to you?" = Restitution. Let's add the next layer: "I will try not to do this again" = Repentance. One way to describe "repentance" is "planned change."

For some people, this is their native language of apology, so this is what they're listening for. Repentance is what convinces them that the apology is sincere, which helps them to let things go and forgive. Without genuine repentance, the other four languages of apology may fall flat. People who have been hurt are wondering, "You say you're sorry, but are you going to turn around and do this again next week? Or will you actually change this time?"

In our research, we repeatedly heard sentiments like this:

"Show me that you're actually willing to change."

"Find a way to stop it from happening again."

"You keep saying you're sorry, but I don't see any improvement. What's your plan?"

"Words aren't enough. I don't want to keep reliving this same issue again."

It's like *Groundhog Day* in relationships, where the same cycle
keeps repeating
over
   and over
     and over
      again,
        and it has to
          STOP.

For many people, this old-school idea of *repentance* is at the heart
of any real apology.

Intention to Change

All true repentance begins in the heart. So if you need to change
a pattern in one of your relationships, it begins with intention. Do
you actually want to change? Do you realize that your choice hurts
someone you care about? Do you want things to be different?

Choose change—and then verbalize it! No more excuses. No more
minimizing the impact of our behavior. No more blame shifting. When
we share that intention to change, we are communicating to the other
person what's brewing inside our brains. They can't see our hearts,
so they have to hear our words. And we have to mean them.

Chase has had a two-year stretch of near-constant conflicts with
his brother. He and his mom joke that his little brother has been in
a tough phase . . . a *two-year* phase. Chase is usually patient with
Jaxon, but honestly he's really tired of having to be the stable one.
After one of Jaxon's bad episodes (which might involve anything from
following him around and hanging on him to making fun of his girlfriend), Jaxon apologizes. For two years, Chase didn't buy the forced
apologies, but then he sensed a shift. "I heard the words, 'I'm sorry,'
but that was always hollow," Chase says. "But last week he told me
that he is going to give me space when I get home from work and not

make fun of my girlfriend anymore. I am finally seeing that he wants to change, and that makes me feel more patient with him. Realistically I don't expect him to be perfect, but I can't stand more of the same."

Change takes time. It's like getting in shape. You don't roll out of bed one morning and decide, "Today I will be in shape." No, it's a process. You force yourself to wake up early, to run even when you don't feel like it, and your fitness grows incrementally. So it is with most relational change.

INTENTION → DISCIPLINE → MINI-SUCCESS → MINI-FAILURE → SIGNS OF PROGRESS → MORE SUCCESS → LASTING CHANGE

Verbalize Your Intent

Some resist the idea of verbalizing their intention to change. "But what if I fail?" they argue. "Won't that just make things worse? Shouldn't I just shut up and make the change?" I see where you're coming from, but the challenge is that the other person can't read your mind. It may take weeks or even months for them to fully observe your changes, and that whole time, they're in turmoil. My advice is that when you apologize, state your intention to change. And mean it. You can even ask them to be patient with you in the process.

But What If I *Won't* Change?

Ah, the old impasse. Let's say you apologize for hurting someone, but honestly, you have no intention of changing. Maybe the person is picking at you for something that's not even morally wrong; they're just too touchy. You've reached a fork in the road.

If you go left: Perhaps you decide that the relationship has reached its natural end. For example, Michael's girlfriend keeps complaining that he doesn't spend enough time with her, but between his family, his two sports, and his academic load, he doesn't have more time. They've had this conversation repeatedly, and the relationship has become drudgery. "Maybe we should just break up," she says, testing him. "I agree," he says. "We can't make this work." In a marriage, you work through tough times, but in a dating relationship, sometimes you just need to move on, so Michael does.

If you go right: You know in your heart that this is a relationship you must save. Maybe you think your sister is too sensitive, but she's clearly in a place where she can't handle your teasing, so you vow to yourself to be more gentle with her. You verbalize that intention to her too: "Sara, I'm not trying to hurt you, but I can see that I did. I'm sorry. I'll try not to do that again. If I slip, will you just tell me, rather than blow up at me?" At this impasse, you choose to turn right, to make a change, simply for the sake of your relationship.

In enduring relationships, sometimes we have to make changes not because of a moral issue but because we love the other person enough to bend a little. Helping my mom carry in groceries? Not a moral issue, but something about it sets her off if I don't, so I can pause my geometry homework to carry in bags. That's a minor sacrifice for relational peace. Driving my little sister to her swim practice? Not a moral issue, but an easy way I can show my family that I'm not self-absorbed (as they've accused). It's twenty minutes of driving that shows my family I'm a changed person.

When you reach the impasse, make a choice. If the relationship is worth saving, then make the change.

What's Your Plan?

Actions speak louder than words. A universal truth, yes?

So if you apologize, and if you intend to change, and if you verbalize that intention to change, and if you will yourself to make the change because this relationship is worth saving—then make a plan and make the change. Do a one-eighty.

You know how you're programmed. Are you the type who needs to write a note on your phone to remind you? I often find that when I write something down and put it in an obvious spot where I'll see it throughout the day, I'm far more likely to get it done. Are you the type who needs to set a time each day to do X? Whether X = text your brother who's struggling in college, or go for a run so you can prove to your coach that you're fit, or do your homework so your mom stops stressing that your grades are so terrible and you'll be living in her basement forever, or _____. Set that alarm on your phone!

Count the Cost

Sometimes change is costly.

Elena and Faith had an easy friendship. For years they seemed inseparable, but when Elena made the varsity cheer team and Faith did not, their lives diverged.

Elena's schedule was overflowing with cheer. Morning lift. Afternoon practice. Friday night game. Repeat. Soon she was so busy with her cheer team and her cheer friends that she hardly had time for Faith.

Meanwhile, Faith wasn't going to just sit at home, so she got a job. Her social life came to a screeching halt. Other than going to school or work, she felt isolated.

Elena would halfheartedly invite Faith to hang out with her on the weekends, but Faith was clearly jealous of Elena's social life and kept saying no. Finally, Faith exploded with resentment. After her outburst, they gave each other the silent treatment for three solid days, and Elena wouldn't even look at her. To her credit, Faith broke the ice, admitted that her expectations of Elena had been unfair, apologized for blaming Elena for her own loneliness, and tried to patch things up. Elena wanted to accept Faith's apology, but she was skeptical: what had changed?

In order for the two girls to move on, they had to make concrete changes. If either of them felt frustrated, they agreed to voice it right away. They agreed that unspoken expectations aren't fair in either direction. They agreed that Faith would come out with Elena at least once a week and that they would start going to the gym together every week. The concrete steps made them both hopeful that the pattern wouldn't repeat itself.

Progress, Not Perfection

What if we fail? What if we're sincerely trying to improve our relationships, and we voice our intention to change, and we're working the plan, but we still sometimes fail?

Well, are we talking about a onetime failure or systemic failure? Are we talking about a micro failure or a nuclear failure?

Back to Elena and Faith's story: Is it possible that some weeks, they won't get the balance quite right? Maybe Elena is out extra, or Faith is feeling insecure, or they just don't communicate as well that week. That doesn't mean their friendship is over. Reset, and keep moving forward. Make progress, but don't expect perfection.

However, what if a husband has a history of physically abusing his wife, apologizes to her, and vows never to hurt her again, but in a fit of rage, he beats her to a pulp? That, my friends, is nuclear failure, and she needs to exit stage left for her own safety.

But most failure isn't of that magnitude, so we need to give ourselves and each other a dose of grace. You can see your sibling/

parent/friend trying, and you can see progress, so don't give up on each other. The tragedy is that people often give up when they are inches from success. Old behavior patterns die slowly. Most people don't expect perfection after an apology, but they do expect effort.

Recap

"I'm sorry" = Regret.

"I was wrong" = Responsibility.

"How can I make it up to you?" = Restitution.

And "I will try not to do this again" = Repentance. For some people, an apology sounds hollow unless they hear in your voice a willingness and intention to change. Language 4, Repentance, can sound like this:

"I know I hurt you, and I don't ever want to do that again. Any ideas on what I could change?"

"Clearly what I'm doing isn't working. What would make this better for you?"

"How could I say that in a different way so that it comes across better?"

"I really do want to change. I know I won't be perfect, but I'm trying. If I revert to my old patterns, will you remind me?"

"I let you down. Again. What would it take for me to start earning your trust back again?"

Reflection

- Is Language 4: Repentance your primary language of apology? To you, do actions mean more than words? When people hurt you, are you looking for evidence of change?

- Why is it so hard for people to change?

- And why is it so hard for us to be patient with people (even with ourselves) while they're in the process of changing?

- When are relationships worth saving? For those, how hard are you willing to fight? When do you need to cut a relationship loose? How can you discern between the two categories?

- What idea(s) will you take away from this chapter to help you better heal your relationships?

SCENE 5

The Language of Request

As the two social media marketing interns at their school, Aliyah and Gabe spend a lot of time together. After school, evenings, weekends—they are always together, creating content, hitting their deadlines, and trying to impress their high-strung, demanding marketing director. Over time, Aliyah is surprised to realize that Gabe is not just her friend; he has become her best friend. Maybe that's half a statement about her friend group and half a statement about how easygoing and fun Gabe is.

There's just one thing about Gabe that bothers Aliyah, though. He never apologizes. Once Aliyah notices the pattern, she sees it all the time. If Gabe makes a mistake, forgets to include her in a text chain, runs over her backpack with his car, whatever, he never actually apologizes. Finally she brings it up.

Gabe listens carefully. His jaw falls open. He blinks. His jaw closes. Slowly he says, "Remember when I forgot to pick up lunch for you last week? I felt like I apologized to you for the inconvenience. What did you need to hear from me?"

"You never asked me to forgive you!" Aaliyah explains.

"So . . . will you forgive me? To me that seems obvious, but . . . it's okay, I can state the obvious." Gabe grins.

"Yes," Aliyah says. Charmed, she smiles. All's right with the world again.

What was Aliyah doing there? She was teaching Gabe how to speak her apology language. She was listening for something specific, so she (finally) told him what she needed to hear in order to fully let it go and move on.

Remember, what one person considers an apology may fall flat for the next person, so we need to speak each other's languages.

LANGUAGE 5

Remember the progression of apologies we've been learning?

"I'm sorry" = Regret.

"I was wrong" = Responsibility.

"How can I make it up to you?" = Restitution.

"I will try not to do this again" = Repentance.

And the grand finale: "Will you forgive me?" This is a humble *request*.

It's obvious that Aliyah's primary apology language is Request. She needs to hear those words: "Will you please forgive me?" To her, that's a sincere apology. She's willing to forgive. In fact, she even wants to forgive Gabe. But she needs to know that Gabe recognizes his need for forgiveness.

In our research we found lots of Aliyahs. We asked respondents, "What do you expect in an apology?" One of every five people said, "I expect the person to ask for my forgiveness." For them, this is the signal of sincerity.

Why does this language matter so much to some people?

First, the words "Will you forgive me?" signal that you want the relationship restored. You don't want any barriers between you. You don't want to gloss over issues. You want an authentic connection.

Second, the words "Will you forgive me?" show that you realize you did something wrong, intentionally or not. You caused the rift between you, so you admit your guilt.

Third, the words "Will you forgive me?" put the power in the other person's hands. You can't force the answer. The person may choose to forgive, or not, and the future of the relationship rests on his or her decision.

Spit It Out

Some people choke over the words "Will you forgive me?" Why are those words so hard for them to spit out?

Fear!

Fear of what?

Fear of losing control. Some people have a high need for control, and relinquishing control makes them feel very uncomfortable, like a full body control freak rash. To ask someone to forgive you means he or she gets to decide (not you!), and subconsciously, you might find that difficult.

Fear of rejection. When you ask, "Will you forgive me?" the other person might say no. To some of us, that feels like a personal rejection, layered on top of a relational conflict, which makes us feel like we have an ulcer.

Fear of failure. To admit I'm wrong might mean I failed the other person, or I even failed myself and betrayed my own values. To some people, admitting "I'm wrong" equates to "I'm a failure." It takes maturity to realize we are not the sum of our worst choices.

Request, Not Demand

Sometimes when we ask for forgiveness, the answer is "not yet." It's hard to wait. But some gaping wounds do not close quickly. We can't demand forgiveness. When we act entitled ("I asked you to forgive me, so move on already"), we show that we don't understand the mini-miracle that forgiveness is. Remember that forgiveness is the choice to release the person from the obligation that resulted from the injury. To pardon the offense. To let go of justice on my terms and entrust it to God's hands and His timing. Forgiveness is an undeserved gift. You can request a gift; you can't demand it.

Let's try an outlandish metaphor here, something that would never happen in real life but helps us grasp the point that emotional healing takes just as long as (if not longer than) physical healing. Let's say you're driving your car with your best friend in the passenger seat. Somehow, despite all your mom's warnings to drive carefully, you manage to crash your car into a tree. Because of the angle of impact, you walk away fine, but your best friend has a badly broken leg. Whose fault here? Yours, 100 percent yours (and the police and your insurance company and your parents agree). But who's paying the higher price? Your best friend. If the next day you show up at her house and ask her to go for a run with you, how's that going to go over? What if you demand it? What if you guilt her into running with you, even though it's going to take time for her leg to heal? That would be absurd, right?

With a physical injury, we can see that the person needs more time to heal. With an emotional injury, the wound may be invisible, but your friend still needs time. Give her the time she needs, and in the meantime, bring her favorite Starbucks drink and watch a movie with her, rather than act impatient that she can't run yet.

Why Is It Hard to Forgive?

I keep telling you that forgiveness is a mini-miracle. Full-blown miracles fall in God's domain; He lets us participate in the minis. Why is it so hard to forgive others?

First, it requires the forgiver to give up his or her quest for justice. At first you may want the offender to "suffer" for what he did. You may argue that he does not "deserve" forgiveness. You're right, he doesn't deserve it. Neither do I. Neither do you. That's what makes this a mini-miracle.

Second, the forgiver may be strapped with long-lasting consequences for the choices someone else made, which isn't fair. For example, a child whose father deserted her may have deep abandonment wounds. That's o percent her fault and 100 percent her dad's fault, but she's the one left scarred in Omaha. She may eventually choose to forgive her dad, but that doesn't erase her feeling lonely and unprotected.

Third, when the wound was deep and/or repeated, the forgiver may really struggle to let it go. Back to the metaphor of the car accident: the girl whose leg was shattered will not pop up and run the next day, or even the next month, or maybe even the next year. Healing takes time. If the wound was shallow, onetime, and more of an accident than "malice aforethought" (Don't you love that phrase? That little gem is in Numbers 35:20 NIV), and if you genuinely apologize in the forgiver's primary language, then the forgiveness may come easily. But if the wound was deep, repeated, and malicious, then that's a hefty minor miracle in the works. Give it time.

Recap

Without the magic words "Will you please forgive me?" your other apology languages—"I'm sorry. I was wrong. I will make it up to you. I'll never do it again"—may sound glib. We all need to learn to speak the language of Request, which can sound like this:

"I'm sorry for how I spoke to you. That came across really rude, and you didn't deserve that. Will you forgive me?"

"I know I hurt you deeply. You have every right to cut me off, but I'm truly sorry for what I did, and I hope you can find it in your heart to forgive me."

"I didn't intend to hurt you, but obviously I did. I

realize that now, and I see that my actions were wrong even though I wasn't trying to hurt you. I promise I won't do that again, and I want to ask you to forgive me."

Reflection

- When someone hurts you, are you listening for those words: "Will you forgive me?"

- The five languages of apology are all equal. One isn't "better" or "more advanced" than the others. So although this one comes last, that doesn't mean it's the most elegant or complex. It just happens to be the fifth, and it just happens to be the wording some people need to hear. Of your closest relationships, who apologizes like this—and by extension, expects you to apologize like this?

- Review the three fears we discussed in this chapter: fear of losing control, fear of rejection, and fear of failure. Which of those fears sometimes wraps its tentacles around you? Why?

- What idea(s) will you take away from this chapter to help you better heal your relationships?

Act 4

MOVING FORWARD

SCENE 1

Healthy + Healing

In the final act of a play, all the pieces start to fall into place. In a tragedy, everybody dies or the kingdom falls apart (sorry, spoiler alert). In a comedy, there's a clever, funny twist. In a romance, the two starstruck characters finally come together. For us, for our purposes in this book about relational conflict, let's circle back to our original purpose: that you would grow through relational conflict and land in a place where you are healthy and healing.

To be human is to be in relationship with others. Don't fall for the modern myth of living as an island, literal or virtual. You need other people. Not just two-dimensional people on a screen. You need three-dimensional, messy relationships with other complex human beings. We all do. God designed us that way. Anytime two imperfect humans are in relationship with each other, we'll inevitably have conflicts of some flavor. The question is not *if* we will have conflicts but *how* we will navigate those conflicts. The immature person writes people off as soon as there's a whiff of imperfection in the other person or in the relationship. The mature person, in contrast, learns how to work through conflict, which is the goal of this book: to equip you to do just that.

Is it easy to address conflict? No, of course not.

Is it effortless to forgive someone who hurt you? No, it's a minor miracle.

Is it natural to make things right, phrasing your apology in the language of the other person? No, it takes effort.

But it's worth it! I'm going to present a premise to you, and I want you to mentally chew on this one for a while:

God's Way Is the Best Way.

I didn't say it's the easiest way. I didn't say it's the path of least resistance. But I can tell you, from my own experience and from talking with thousands of clients in my office, that God's way is best for us.

Remember that the Creator custom designed you, and He knows how you function best. The manual He wrote for your life, the Bible, isn't some dead, dusty tome. His words give you life. When He tells us to forgive others and to make things right when we can, He's setting us free from the acid of unforgiveness and the weight of broken relationships.

Is it hard? Yes, but you can do hard things, and when you choose to do hard things in the short-term, you make your life much easier in the long-term. God says,

> Now what I am commanding you today is not too difficult for you or beyond your reach. It is not up in heaven, so that you have to ask, "Who will ascend into heaven to get it and proclaim it to us so we may obey it?" Nor is it beyond the sea, so that you have to ask, "Who will cross the sea to get it and proclaim it to us so we may obey it?" No, the word is very near you; it is in your mouth and in your heart so you may obey it. See, I set before you today life and prosperity, death and destruction. . . . **Now choose life**. (Deuteronomy 30:11–15, 19 NIV, emphasis added)

Now choose life in your relationships. Forgive! Let the little things go. Address the big things directly. Do what you can to make things right with others. "If it is possible, as far as it depends on you, live at peace with everyone" (Romans 12:18 NIV).

And you will reap the rewards, for God's way is always best.

Reflection

- In your opinion, are there any perfect endings in life: "And they all lived happily ever after"? Why or why not?

- Can you think of a time in your life when a conflict actually made your relationship stronger?

- When we forgive, it feels as if we're doing the other person (the offender) a favor. In what way is the choice to forgive the offender actually a favor to yourself?

- Reread Romans 12:18 (NIV): "If it is possible, as far as it depends on you, live at peace with everyone." What do you think that caveat "as far as it depends on you" means? Which dynamics can you control? Which ones are out of your control?

- Deep down, do you believe the premise that God's way is always best? Why or why not? How could choosing to accept that revolutionary premise set you free?

- In what relationship do you need to "choose life"?

SCENE 2

Letting Go

Born four minutes apart, Skylar and Andres have shared most experiences in life. Same birthday, same parents, same gene pool, same childhood house, same school, same hair color, same experiences, largely. But by the age of seventeen, the twins couldn't be more different.

When their parents divorced, it broke something inside both of them. Their mom and dad did their best to give them stability and opportunity. They even got them into counseling, which helped both of them process the rupture in their family. Andres seemed to heal from those initial wounds, but Skylar never did.

Andres moves through the world lightly. His mom has often joked that he has the memory of a goldfish. Maybe it's his happy-go-lucky personality. But this isn't really an intelligence or memory issue; the twins have nearly identical IQs. Somehow Andres was able to process his loss and then let it go.

Skylar never did. She's popular and has a lot of "friends," but she doesn't let anyone get close to her, except Andres, and she doesn't trust anyone, except Andres. When her therapist asks her directly, she says she has forgiven her parents but that she will never forget that her mom left and her dad passively watched it happen. "True," Dr. Winters said. "You will never truly forget. But Skylar, you have to let go."

Through the past three acts, we've explored ways to make things right when conflict inevitably arises in our relationships. Whatever the nature of the conflict, whoever is involved, we cannot fully resolve it until we're able to let go of hurt, anger, fear, bitterness, and the other negative emotions that grip our hearts. That process of letting go—releasing the desire for revenge or even justice—is, in the eyes of most mental health experts, foundational to moving on in your life. That process of letting go is complex and messy, so let's break it down.

But first, what if we don't let things go?

The obvious external result is that the relationship stays broken. Every time you interact with the person, it's uncomfortable for you, and it's likely uncomfortable for everyone else in the vicinity too.

The obvious internal result is that you stay broken. Anger brews into resentment and bitterness. You might obsess over the offense, replaying it in your mind. You might have mental arguments with the person. You might spend a lot of energy avoiding him or her. You might feel tempted to gossip or get even. You might radiate negative energy. Ultimately, you might make yourself miserable.

What Letting Go Is *Not*

Before we define what letting go means, let's describe what it isn't.

Letting go ≠ excusing or diminishing the person's behavior. You shouldn't say, "That's okay," when it's clearly not. You shouldn't say, "It's no big deal," or "Don't worry about it." You are not absolving them of the responsibility for their choices.

Letting go ≠ forgetting what was done to you. Everything that's happened to you impresses on your mind/soul/body in some way, even if the memory isn't in the forefront of your conscious thought. Sometimes it's embedded in your subconscious. Sometimes, even after you've chosen to forgive someone, the past will resurface, and you have to choose to forgive him again.

Just as letting go does not erase your memories, so letting go also doesn't erase your emotions. When painful memories resurface, your emotions may sweep back over you. That's normal. You may feel a resurgence of that initial anger, or hurt, or disappointment—whatever words you give to it—and when that happens, tell yourself, "Yes, I remember the offense. Yes, it hurts again, but I'm not going to let it control me."

Letting go ≠ removing all the consequences of poor choices. A client once said to me, "Dr. Chapman, to be honest, I forgave him. But I still don't trust him."

And I replied, "Welcome to the human race."

Remember our formula from Act 3? Forgiveness ≠ restitution. For your own peace, you have to let the offense go, but sometimes it's not wise or safe to rebuild the relationship. You can forgive and keep your distance. Forgiveness does not automatically rebuild trust and restore relationships, but without forgiveness, there's no hope for restoration.

Some people have unrealistic expectations. They think, "If I apologize, then everything will be as good as new." Here's an illustration. Imagine a beach house. A well-loved, right-on-the-beach, family vacation home. The beach in front of it keeps eroding year by year, and then the unthinkable: a hurricane rips through the town. Even though the family safely evacuated, the house sustains serious damage from the beating waves and hurricane force winds. The owners begin the grueling process of restoration, rebuilding the deck that was torn off and gutting the entire first floor, which had been flooded. After two years of construction, the new house is beautiful, but not the same beautiful. So it is with relationships. When we damage them severely, we can choose to rebuild them, but they may never look quite the same. That's life.

What if someone hurts you but never apologizes or shows remorse? That makes forgiveness harder, and that makes restoration impossible, but you can still let go and move on.

What Letting Go Entails

Letting go doesn't happen instantaneously. We need to remind ourselves that it is a *process*, not a onetime fix.

Let's look at three components, or steps, to the process of letting go.

Step 1: Acknowledge the other person's humanity. I'm human, you're human, and so is the person who hurt you. We are all broken and fallible. We are hurting people who hurt people. We all make mistakes. We all have besetting sins, meaning deep-seated character flaws that bite us again and again, e.g., impatience or impulsivity. The first step in letting go is seeing the humanity in the person who hurt you.

Step 2 (and this one's a beast): Surrender your right to get even. Give up your desire to see bad things happen to that person. Release your longing for the person to get what he deserves. Remember, this step doesn't mean that what he did to you is okay; it means that you will be okay. Release the person who hurt you to God, letting God take care of that person rather than insisting on justice on your own terms.

Step 3: Revise your feelings toward the person. This takes time. You might argue, "But I can't change my feelings. They are what they are." True, *but*. The key here is to change the statements you say to yourself about the other person. For example, "Yes, Mia humiliated me in front of others, but I want to move on. When I see her, I don't want to see *that*; I want to see *her*." You do not allow your mind to be obsessed with past failures that are now forgiven. You are choosing to let the past go, not let it control you.

Who Wins?

"But if I choose to forgive and let this go, doesn't that let the other person win?"

Is the answer obvious to you yet? When you choose to give up your right to get even, you win. You live at peace. You sleep better. You clear out your mental space for things that actually matter. You heal, and often emotional/psychological healing has physical components too (e.g., absence of headaches, nausea, muscle pain). You are able to see and experience the good things in your life, without your vision clouded by the pain of the past.

When you forgive, you win.

The Only Way

Unfortunately, being alive on this planet involves conflict, challenges, disappointments, and difficult people. Ultimately, I would argue, letting go is the only way to survive with your sanity and heart intact. The alternatives are miserable: living in a prison of unforgiveness, hurt, and hate. I don't recommend it.

Reflection

- Is there a situation you've had a hard time letting go of? Review the three steps. Where are you stuck? Why?

- Why is it essential for us to acknowledge that forgiveness and letting go are a *process*, not a onetime fix?

- Sometimes we feel pressure by others to let things go before we've had time to process them. Have you ever felt pressured this way?

- What helps you to let go and move on?

- What burdens of unforgiveness are you trying to carry through your life?

Rebuilding Trust

Life demands trust. You trust that the mechanic installed your new brakes correctly. You trust that the nurse is giving you your tetanus booster, not some experimental drug. You trust that your chicken sandwich was cooked to a minimum of 165 degrees so you don't get food poisoning.

Relationships demand trust. You trust that your friend has your best interests at heart. You trust that your coach is trying to develop your skills. You trust that your math teacher is teaching you trig correctly.

In our culture, trust is often fractured, if not outright shattered. People have lost trust in institutions: Big Tech, Big Pharma, the government, mainstream media, elite academia, etc. That general malaise of mistrust seeps into other areas of our lives, making us more cautious, skeptical, and cynical.

The issue of trust is not as clear-cut as we might imagine. We often think in extreme terms: someone is either "totally trustworthy" or "totally untrustworthy." The reality is that most people can be appropriately trusted in some contexts. Trust exists on a spectrum. The person you trust most might be your dad, the person you trust least might be your ex-boyfriend, and like dots scattered on a graph are all the other people in your life, who are trustworthy to some extent in some contexts.

See, trust depends on the situation. You might trust an Uber driver to deliver you to the airport, but you wouldn't give him your login and password to your bank account. You might trust your dad to pay your college tuition bill but not to keep a low profile during Parents' Weekend. (You know him and his embarrassing quirks all too well.) You might trust your teammate Marshall to score the winning goal if you pass to him, but you wouldn't trust him not to steal your phone charger and snacks in the hotel when you're not looking.

Are You Trustworthy?

Before you hold others to an unrealistic standard, do some honest self-assessment: Would you trust you? Are you a trustworthy person? Are you who you profess to be? Do you follow through?

Some timeless advice: Let your *yes* mean *yes*. If you know you won't do something, then don't volunteer for it. If you have no spare time on Tuesday night, then don't offer to create the presentation on Google Slides for your history group project that's due on Wednesday. It's better to disappoint your team on Monday than to let them down on Wednesday when the stakes are high.

Rebuilding Trust

What if you trusted someone, and he let you down, stabbed you in the back, or broke your heart? Now we're in some complicated territory. Even when we've done our best to make things right in a damaged relationship, the relationship may still be in ruins.

If you're committed to restoring the relationship, then you have serious work to do:

> *If you were the one in the wrong*, then after you have apologized in the other person's native language, you need to *consistently* show up and prove that you can be trusted again. You may need to show up 99 times before the person trusts you with the 100th. You also have to give the other person time to slowly begin to trust you again.

If you were the one wronged, and you're ready to restore the relationship, then you will have to take the risk of trusting again—in tiny, incremental steps. With an open mind and an eagle eye, you watch as he proves over time that he can be trusted with little things. Only then can you cautiously begin to trust him with slightly bigger things. Look for evidence of heart change, not perfection.

Let me illustrate. Riley, Lucia, and Leah were best friends for three years. They were the inseparable trio. At the end of sophomore year, something invisible shifted. Riley and Lucia started spending more time together, and Leah started spending more time with her boyfriend, whom the other two resented. And they didn't hide the fact that they resented him and the time he spent with Leah. Their silent glares morphed into critical words, gossip, and nasty rumors. Leah heard the rumors from a mutual acquaintance, and her friends' words hurt. Nothing hurts quite as much as the wounds from your so-called best friends.

Finally Leah found the courage to confront them directly (good for her!), and to their credit, they listened (good for them!). They empathized and apologized, and they asked what they could do to restore the friendship.

Did Leah forgive them? Yes, but that was months ago, and she's still a little on edge. Every time they make silent eye contact, or whisper quietly, or start to make plans without her, Leah's doubts resurface. It may take them a full year to regain the ground they lost. But to all three of them, it's worth it.

Reflection

- Trust exists on a continuum. Describe what that continuum looks like in your relationships.

- After you're wounded in a personal relationship, why is it so hard to trust again? Describe a strained relationship where you had to work to rebuild trust.

- Describe a strained relationship where you need to work to rebuild trust.

Backstage

QUIZ, APOLOGY CHEAT SHEET,
VERSES TO MEMORIZE,
ABOUT THE AUTHORS

Quiz

S o what is *your* natural apology language? It's always helpful to understand yourself before you attempt to understand another human being. Take the quiz below or online for insights into your native language of apology.

For a free online quiz
please visit:

5lovelanguages.com

Context

The following assessment is designed to help you discover your apology language. Read each of the twenty-five hypothetical scenarios and choose the **one** response you would most like to hear if you were living that scenario. In each case, assume that you and the other person have a relationship and that it's in your best interest to maintain that relationship—meaning, if the other person damaged your relationship, assume it's worth it to you to receive the apology. Also assume that the offender is aware of his or her offense because you have already had a conversation in which you expressed your hurt in a direct way.

Note that some of the possible responses to each of the twenty-five scenarios will sound a little similar. Focus less on the overlap and more on which response *most* appeals to you, and then move on to the next item. Don't overthink it; go by instinct. Allow ten to fifteen minutes to complete the profile. Relax, and don't rush.

Start

Think of a specific time when you dealt with an offense and wanted to mend the relationship. Hold that experience in your head as you consider the following twenty-five paired statements. Circle the letter next to the statement that better describes what would sound meaningful to you in an apology. Neither statement may be a perfect fit for you or the experience in your mind but choose the statement that captures the essence of what is most meaningful to you, most of the time.

1. **It's more meaningful to me when I hear someone say . . .**

    A "I deeply regret embarrassing you as I did."

    E "Our friendship is so important to me. Will you please forgive me?"

2. **It's more meaningful to me when someone says . . .**

    B "I admit it—I made a big mistake."

    D "I want to grow from this experience. Would you help me figure out steps to handle this type of thing better?"

3. **It's more meaningful to me when someone tells me . . .**

    C "What can I do or say to make things right between us?"

    B "I had a bad attitude, and it showed. I should have thought more about what I was doing."

4. **It's more meaningful to me when someone says . . .**

    D "I don't want to do this again, so I will come up with ways to avoid mistakes like this in the future."

E "I apologize for my actions. You obviously don't have to forgive me, but I hope you will."

5.   It's more meaningful to me when someone asks me . . .

E "Can you possibly forgive me?"

C "What can I do to mend our relationship?"

6.   It's more meaningful to me when I hear someone say . . .

B "My fault entirely. I could make excuses, but really, I have no good excuse for my actions."

E "You have every right to hold this against me, but will you consider forgiving me?"

7.   It's more meaningful to me when someone asks me . . .

C "I'd like to make things better between us. What can I do to make things right?"

E "You don't have to answer immediately, but will you consider forgiving me for this mistake?"

8.   It's more meaningful to me when I hear these words from someone . . .

E "I want to ask you to forgive me."

A "It hurts me to see you hurting like this."

9.   It's more meaningful to me when someone says . . .

B "I really messed up this time. Our whole team failed because of me."

C "Can we back up and let me try to fix this? I really want to repair the damage I caused."

10. **It's more meaningful to me when I hear someone say . . .**

     A "I'm furious with myself over how I handled this. I cringe when I remember the way I acted."

     D "I know that what I've been doing is not helpful. What would you like to see me change that would make this better for you?"

11. **It's more meaningful to me when someone tells me . . .**

     B "I know what I did was wrong."

     A "I'm so sorry. I feel terrible that I let you down."

12. **It's more meaningful to me when someone asks me . . .**

     D "What changes could I put into place so that you might start to trust me again in the future?"

     E "I hope this won't permanently damage our relationship. Will you please accept my apology?"

13. **It's more meaningful to me when someone says . . .**

     A "I can see that my actions hurt you, and I feel terrible about what I did."

     C "Is there anything I can do to repair the damage I've done?"

14. **It's more meaningful to me when someone tells me . . .**

     B "If I'd thought through what I was doing, I would have realized it was wrong."

     E "I know I've caused you a significant amount of trouble. I would really appreciate it if you'd forgive me."

15. **It's more meaningful to me when I hear someone say . . .**

     A "I am truly sorry for my actions plus the ways they affected you."

D "If I'm ever upset with you again, I promise to approach you directly to talk it through."

16. **It's more meaningful to me when someone says . . .**

    E "I hope you can find it in your heart to forgive me."

    B "I absolutely should not have done that."

17. **It's more meaningful to me when I hear someone say . . .**

    D "Talk is cheap. I'll work to show you that I'm changing."

    C "Is there anything I can do to make up for what I did?"

18. **It's more meaningful to me when someone tells me . . .**

    A "I'm embarrassed by my behavior, and I'm so sorry."

    B "No excuses. I admit I was wrong."

19. **It's more meaningful to me when I hear someone say . . .**

    E "I apologize. Will you please forgive me?"

    D "Going forward, I will manage my time and prioritize better so that I won't make the same mistake."

20. **It's more meaningful to me when someone says . . .**

    D "I hope I never do this again. Let's talk about what I can do better in the future."

    C "It doesn't feel like it's enough to just say, 'My bad.' How can I make this up to you?"

21. **It's more meaningful to me when someone tells me . . .**

    B "I know that my actions were totally unacceptable. I own that."

    A "It stresses me out to know that you had to stand there waiting on me. I regret frustrating you."

22. It's more meaningful to me when someone says . . .

    C "I know I've inconvenienced you. What can I do for you that could help balance things out?"

    A "I'm unhappy with how I've hurt you. I'm so disappointed in myself."

23. It's more meaningful to me when I hear these words from someone . . .

    C "What can I do to make this situation right for you—immediately?"

    D "It may take time for me to earn your trust back, but in the process, I hope you see changes in me so you know you can trust me."

24. It's more meaningful to me when someone says . . .

    A "I'm so sorry about that. I feel awful that I disappointed you."

    C "Saying 'I'm sorry' doesn't feel like enough. What more can I say or do to make this up to you?"

25. It's more meaningful to me when someone says . . .

    D "Everything I've learned from this experience will prevent me from making that same mistake again."

    B "I know what I did was inappropriate—no excuses."

Scoring

Now go back and count the number of times you circled each individual letter and write that number in the blank beside that letter.

    _____ A = Language 1: *Regret*

    _____ B = Language 2: *Responsibility*

    _____ C = Language 3: *Restitution*

    _____ D = Language 4: *Repentance*

    _____ E = Language 5: *Request*

Results

The highest possible score for any single apology language is ten. Which language had your highest score? This is your primary apology language. If two languages tied for you, then congratulations, you're bilingual: you have two equally dominant apology languages. If you have a second language that scored really close to your primary score, then that means you have a secondary apology language, and both languages are meaningful to you.

Now what? Self-knowledge is powerful, but applying that to your relationships is a game changer. Read back through the chapter about your primary language closely to understand how it affects your relationships.

Disclaimer (The Fine Print)

Is this a perfect tool? No! And some smart readers figure out how to manipulate it. No lifetime warranty or money-back guarantee on this quiz; it's a tool. This assessment is not intended as a substitute for any medical or psychiatric advice, diagnosis, or treatment you need. If you have questions, direct them to a licensed clinician. The use of this quiz does not create an express or implied professional relationship with the authors. Any actions taken as a result of using this assessment are at the sole discretion of the user, and the authors and publishers are not liable or responsible for any actions taken due to the use of this assessment. Translation: Legal jargon for this wacky world in which we live. Use the tool, but don't stake your life on it.

Apology Cheat Sheet

What NOT to Say When You Apologize
"Haven't you gotten over that yet?"
"I am sorry that you were offended."
"I should be excused because I . . ."
"You're too sensitive. I was only joking."
"What's the big deal?"
"Give me a break."
"You just need to get over it."
"Well, there's nothing I can do about that now. I can't change the past."

What TO Say When You Apologize

"I'd like to circle back to (name the issue). I realize I didn't say (or do) things the right way, and I apologize for that."

"I am so sorry."

"I did it, and I have no excuse."

"I've damaged your trust."

"I was careless, insensitive, thoughtless, or rude."

"I will do the work to fix my mistake going forward."

"You have every right to be upset."

"My mistake is part of a pattern I need to change. I promise I'll work on it."

"I will rebuild your trust by . . ."

"I've put you in a very difficult position."

"I know that I need to show you how I will change."

"Will you please forgive me?"

Verses to Memorize

We live in a look-it-up culture. Who won the 2010 Super Bowl? Look it up. What's the best route to drive to the game? Look it up. How do I calculate my GPA? Look it up.

For lots of the quick info we use during the day, that's a stellar approach. You can keep your mental space clear by letting your iPhone do the grinding work in the moment. However, that approach does not work in the relational domain. We need God's Word embedded in our minds and hearts so that in the moment, the Holy Spirit can prompt us with the truths we need in the moment.

For those readers who look to the Bible for guidance on relationships, you can pick a few favorite verses below to tattoo on your brain. To help you memorize them, write them in a prominent place where you'll see them, whether that's your screen saver on your phone, a note on your laptop, or an index card on your bathroom mirror. We need these regular reminders so that when relational conflicts arise, the first thing we see is not social media but a timeless principle from God's Word. The verses below are all from the New International Version.

DRAMA

"Blessed are the peacemakers, for they will be called children of God" (Matthew 5:9).

"If it is possible, as far as it depends on you, live at peace with everyone" (Romans 12:18).

"Do not take revenge, my dear friends, but leave room for God's wrath, for it is written: 'It is mine to avenge; I will repay,' says the Lord" (Romans 12:19).

ANGER

"'In your anger do not sin': Do not let the sun go down while you are still angry" (Ephesians 4:26).

"Fools give full vent to their rage, but the wise bring calm in the end" (Proverbs 29:11).

"A quick-tempered person does foolish things, and the one who devises evil schemes is hated" (Proverbs 14:17).

FORGIVENESS

"Whoever would foster love covers over an offense, but whoever repeats the matter separates close friends" (Proverbs 17:9).

"Bear with each other and forgive one another if any of you has a grievance against someone. Forgive as the Lord forgave you" (Colossians 3:13).

WORDS

"Sin is not ended by multiplying words, but the prudent hold their tongues" (Proverbs 10:19).

"The words of the reckless pierce like swords, but the tongue of the wise brings healing" (Proverbs 12:18).

"Without wood a fire goes out; without a gossip a quarrel dies down" (Proverbs 26:20).

LISTENING

"To answer before listening—that is folly and shame" (Proverbs 18:13).

"My dear brothers and sisters, take note of this: Everyone should be quick to listen, slow to speak and slow to become angry" (James 1:19).

"The way of fools seems right to them, but the wise listen to advice" (Proverbs 12:15).

FREEDOM

"It is for freedom that Christ has set us free. Stand firm, then, and do not let yourselves be burdened again by a yoke of slavery" (Galatians 5:1).

"I have come that they may have life, and have it to the full" (John 10:10b).

"So if the Son sets you free, you will be free indeed" (John 8:36).

ABOUT THE AUTHORS

The authors' own understanding of forgiveness has been shaped by the late Dr. Lewis Smedes's seminal text, *Forgive and Forget* (HarperCollins, 2007), a revolutionary and freeing treatise on the centrality of forgiveness.

Gary Chapman has decades of experience as a marriage and family counselor, a minister, conference speaker, radio host, and is a prolific author, well known for the 5 Love Languages® series, including *The 5 Love Languages of Teenagers*, *A Teen's Guide to the 5 Love Languages*, and many more.

Jennifer Thomas is a business consultant, psychologist, and TEDx speaker. Jennifer developed the concept of apology languages. She and Dr. Chapman coauthored *When Sorry Isn't Enough*, applying research they conducted for their book *The 5 Apology Languages*. Jennifer gives keynote presentations on both the 5 Love Languages® and the 5 Apology Languages. She can be found at www.drjenthomas.com.

Paige Haley Drygas has worked in publishing as a writer and editor for nearly three decades. She served as the general editor of *True Images: The Bible for Teen Girls* and *True Identity: The Bible for Women*.

In one of her past lives she led Peachtree Publishing Services, the premier Bible proofreading company. In her current incarnation she teaches high school English and spends her days happily surrounded by teens: her 112 students and her two teenage sons. She lives with her husband and their sons in Frisco, Texas.

THE SECRET TO GREAT RELATIONSHIPS— JUST FOR TEENS

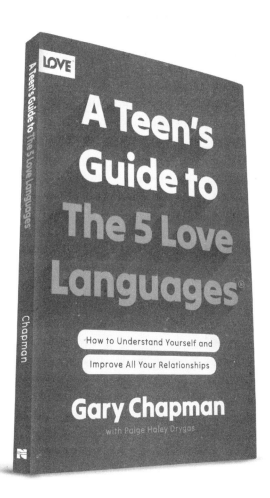

LOVE

A Teen's Guide to The 5 Love Languages

A Teen's Guide to The 5 Love Languages®

How to Understand Yourself and

Improve All Your Relationships

Gary Chapman

with Paige Haley Drygas

Chapman

Derived from the original #1 *New York Times* bestseller, *A Teen's Guide to the 5 Love Languages* is the first-ever edition written just to teens, *for* teens, and with a teen's world in mind. It guides emerging adults in discovering and understanding their own love languages as well as how to best express love to others.

Also available as an eBook